Neurobrand**ing**

• • •

Strategies for shaping consumer behavior

Dr Peter Steidl

Dr Peter Steidl has asserted his right under the Copyright, Designs and Patents Act 1988 to be identified as the author of this work.

This book is sold subject to the condition that it shall not, by way of trade or otherwise, be lent, resold, hired out, or otherwise circulated without the author's prior consent in any form of binding or cover other than that in which it is published and without a similar condition, including this condition, being imposed on subsequent purchasers. No part of this book may be reproduced in any manner whatsoever without written permission except in the case of brief quotations embodied in critical articles and reviews.

Limit of Liability/Disclaimer of Warranty: While the author has used his best efforts in preparing this book, he makes no representations or warranties with respect to the accuracy or completeness of the contents of this book and specifically disclaims any implied warranties or merchantability or fitness for a particular purpose. The advice and strategies contained herein may not be suitable for your situation. You should consult with a professional where appropriate. The author shall not be liable for any loss of profit or any other commercial damages, including but not limited to special, incidental, consequential, or other damages.

For information email Dr Peter Steidl at
peter@neurothinking.com

Copyright © 2018 Dr Peter Steidl
All rights reserved.

ISBN-13: 978-1717146199
ISBN-10: 1717146198

The Neuromarketing Science & Business Association (NMSBA) Neuromarketing Publication Series

Brain research, typically appearing under the heading of *neuroscience* or *cognitive science*, has provided us with unprecedented insights into how the human brain works. Neuromarketing brings together and sometimes reinterprets neuroscience findings that are particularly relevant to the field of marketing, creating a new practice.

Neuromarketing touches on all aspects of marketing, from marketing and brand strategy to creative execution, above the line and social media, shopper marketing, package and product design and innovation, and literally anything else a marketer might consider or do. The reason is obvious: all these activities are designed to impact on the consumer's mind – to change the way they feel about the brand, to increase the likelihood of purchase, and even to shape the consumption or usage experience.

It follows that there are many different topics to address when looking at the area of neuromarketing, but all these themes share common ground: understanding and shaping how consumers feel, think and act.

The NMSBA Neuromarketing Series addresses the specialised needs of anyone who leads or supports the marketing effort, including the agencies that often provide essential services in strategy, creative, research and implementation. The Series allows you to select the topics you want to know more about without having to wade through hundreds of pages of material that may be interesting, but ultimately irrelevant to your particular area of responsibility.

We are always interested in constructive comments and suggestions. Please do email us if you have suggestions for future publications, if you are aware of promising new developments, or want to contribute to this Publication Series.

Carla Nagel
Executive Director, NMSBA
carla@nmsba.com

Contents

Setting the Scene 7

Part I: The neuroscience foundation 12

1. Memories 14
2. Goals 24
3. Context 36
4. A roadmap of the consumer's mind 43
5. Habitual buying: driven by memories 46

Part II: Strategic considerations 61

6. SWOT Exploration: identifying high-level strategic options 66
7. Defining the strategic direction across your brand portfolio 74
8. Disruption strategies 85
   - 8.1 Blue Ocean strategy 88
   - 8.2 Cultural Disruption 96
   - 8.3 Radically innovating what things mean 109
   - 8.4 Developing a higher-level emotional relationship 118
   - 8.5 How extreme should your disruption be? 130
9. Disrupting categorizations 132
10. Brand Vision Archetypes 137
11. Strategic segmentation 147

Part III: Execution 159

12 Marketing communications 161

13 Shopper marketing and the Path-to-Purchase 197

14 Packaging design 219

15 Big Data and neuroscience – a marriage made in heaven? 229

16 Organizational issues 232

17 Getting ready for the future: Artificial Intelligence 237

About the author 241

References 242

Setting the scene

Undoubtedly you are aware of the technological revolution that is gathering pace. Artificial intelligence, robotics, blockchain, autonomous cars, drones, 3D printing and other technologies are swiftly changing the marketing and competitive landscape. As a marketer you will face two major challenges: first, an increasingly large number of jobless consumers, and secondly, technologies that insert themselves as intermediaries between the consumer and your brand.

The World Bank, the Oxford Martin Institute in collaboration with Citi, McKinsey & Co and other credible parties have all undertaken detailed assessments of today's jobs, evaluating to what extent technologies that are already being deployed today or are in advanced stages of development could beneficially replace components of these jobs, or even take over the whole job. The resulting prediction is that, on average, close to 50% of today's jobs will disappear.

What is less clear is how long it will take for this new industrial revolution to happen. There will naturally be differences in acceptance rates across countries, and some environments will facilitate faster adoption of new technologies than others. For example, Singapore's well-organized road system will be able to accommodate autonomous cars more readily than, say, Indonesia's or India's, and replacement cycles will introduce natural delays in the adoption of some technologies.

At the same time it is probable that relatively few new jobs will be created. Here is just one example: VOEST, the Austrian steelworks, recently commissioned a new plant that will produce 500,000 tons of steel a year. A traditional plant with this capacity would provide up to 1,000 jobs, but new technology will allow this plant to be operated by some 14 employees. And if the demand for their steel doubles? It might mean another 14 jobs. We now live in a time when technology creates jobs for technologies, and even a dramatic increase in demand will not lead to a massive increase in employment in technology-rich industries.

An important difference to past industrial revolutions is that this time thinking jobs will be replaced, not just manual labor. Richard and Daniel Susskind have analyzed eight professions in great depth (including management consulting) and concluded *"We expect an 'incremental transformation' in the way that we produce and distribute expertise in society. This will lead eventually to a dismantling of the traditional professions."*[1]

Arguably we should not even call this revolution an 'industrial revolution' as it is by no means limited to the supply side, i.e., the work environment. Rather, we are already seeing signs of massive changes in the way we live that will have a dramatic impact on demand as well. The advent of digital home and personal assistants, the Internet of Things (IoT), self-monitoring devices, the change from the written word to voice in many applications and gadgets are all changing the way we live, impacting on the products and services we are likely to desire in the future and how we will acquire them.

When it comes to dealing with this avalanche of mass unemployment governments, driven as always by a desire to keep things simple rather than to make it work, seem to prefer the idea of adopting a Universal Basic Income (UBI). The concept is great – it is a much more dignified, less bureaucratic way of supporting the unemployed than most current unemployment schemes. All citizens are guaranteed a base level of income and unemployed people are entitled to the UBI regardless of whether they pick up some casual work, they don't have to prove that they are applying for jobs, and they don't have to turn up at a counter to be grilled by government employees.

However, the problem is that the UBI – at least, as it is being tested today in various pilots around the world – is

---

[1] Richard Susskind & Daniel Susskind, *The Future of the Professions*, Oxford University Press, 2015

typically based on providing somewhere around 20 percent of the average income. Some proponents of this inadequate approach suggest that the UBI could be raised at some future stage, but fail to explain where the extra money would come from.

As a marketer you won't find it difficult to imagine what would happen if, say, a third of consumers are on the UBI earning about as much as someone on today's level of unemployment benefits.

These scenarios will take some years to play out. But another major technological development is already starting to make an impact: the introduction of the digital home or personal assistant. While Amazon and Google are currently in leading positions in this market Apple, Microsoft, Alibaba and others are all trying to gain a significant share.

The impact of the home assistant on shopping behavior will vary. Consumers are not likely to delegate purchases they enjoy making themselves, where exploring options and selecting the product or brand is an important part of the total experience. At the other extreme, however, many grocery items are already bought out of habit rather than brand loyalty or preference, and early experiences in the US have shown that many consumers don't ask for a specific brand when they instruct their home assistant to buy on their behalf. None of this should come as a surprise, given that discount grocery chains like Aldi had no difficulty switching consumers to their house brands from the brands they used to buy habitually.

Given current trends and developments I believe you should expect the perfect storm:
- The technological revolution will lead to massive unemployment.
- The UBI is currently the solution preferred by governments and the tech sector.
- The UBI (or a continuation of paying unemployment benefits) will lead to a massive decline in consumer spending and create a highly price-sensitive market.

- Price-sensitive consumers are likely to delegate shopping to their digital assistant, instructing it to look for the most price-competitive offer.

This leaves two core strategies open to retailers and brand owners:
1. Become the *price leader* – an option that is not feasible for many retailers and brand owners.
2. Develop a *strong emotional relationship* between the consumer and your brand which will encourage the consumer to shop rather than delegate the shopping task or, if delegating, to specify their preferred retailer or brand.

The crucial point is this: at no other time has an effective brand strategy been more important, and at no other time has a brand's agility been a greater indicator of likely prosperity and even survival in the emerging environment. In the short- to medium-term the strength of your brand will determine if the shopper asks for it by name when briefing their digital assistant. In the medium- to long-term your brand has an even more challenging task: to become a permissible indulgence, a preferred brand that consumers won't give up easily even when they find themselves living on a paltry UBI.

While all this is quite obvious, it is not clear how brands can form a strong, meaningful relationship with consumers that will protect them in a technology-driven future where digital assistants have the power to place orders that favor particular retailers or brands.

As a marketer you will need to address a number of key challenges, including:
- How will consumer behavior change when a third of the population is unemployed?
- How will you boost the likelihood that your brand is specified when the consumer delegates purchases to a digital home assistant?
- How can you adjust your offer and your brand's positioning to be relevant and desirable in the emerging new operating environment?

Specific strategic considerations include:
- If you can't be the price leader (and, by definition, the vast majority of brands can't) then the only way to succeed in this environment is to build a strong emotional relationship with the consumer.
- To start with, you need to develop a clear brand positioning that allows the consumer to understand which of their goals your brand addresses.
- But you also need to develop a strong emotional relationship with consumers as familiarity, buying habits and even impulse buying will no longer drive purchases to the extent they do today.
- This means that you need to move from simply exposing consumers to your offer and messages to engaging them.
- As it will take several years to build such a relationship you need to start now, rather than wait until major technological disruption has totally changed your operating environment, putting you on the back foot and limiting your ability to shape how consumers feel about your brand because they are too busy with their own survival.

This book will help you to address these – and other – brand strategy challenges.

Finally, please keep in mind that this book has been written for readers who have a basic neuromarketing foundation, allowing me to present neurobranding strategies and tools without detailed discussion of the underlying concepts. While I provide a brief overview on the most important concepts in Part I, if you are new to this field I recommend you read my book *'Neuromarketing Essentials: What Every Marketer Needs to Know'* or another introductory publication, and then return to this book.

PART 1
The neuroscience foundation

Why do consumers spend money on things they don't need? Why do they replace things that are perfectly functional and fit-for-use with something that is newer, better, more impressive or more popular? What is it that drives them to do these and other, seemingly irrational, things?

The answer is the neurotransmitter dopamine, sometimes also called the 'feel-good' neurotransmitter.

The human mind is designed to seek happiness. Yet despite our hardwired tendency to look for happiness we still find it difficult to experience happiness, especially over an extended period of time. How is this possible? The problem is that our mind drives us to seek *happiness, but it is not designed to make us* feel *happy.*

Here's how it works: when you have a positive experience your nonconscious mind releases dopamine, and that makes you feel happy. But your dopamine level declines rapidly and you naturally want to repeat the great feeling of happiness, so you seek out another dopamine hit. You can get that dopamine hit either by repeating an experience that delivered it in the past, or you can try something else you expect to deliver.

However, as you get used to particular experiences the dopamine hit they deliver becomes less and less powerful, because they become predictable and don't deliver the excitement they used to. For example, experiencing a virtual reality game for the first time will likely deliver a big dopamine hit, but after a number of repeat plays you will find the experience less compelling and will seek out new games that deliver stronger dopamine hits.

A final point that is really important is that dopamine is also released when you expect *future rewards, not just when you actually experience them. This means that you are driven to repeat experiences or find promising new ones that you expect to trigger a dopamine hit.*

Managing dopamine is fundamental to marketing and we will come across the powerful impact of dopamine many times as we explore the area of neurobranding.

So if dopamine is what drives the consumer to act, what determines their brand choice? If you want to shape consumer behavior you will need to – first and foremost – understand the key factors that determine the choices they make. These are shown in the following diagram: memories, goals and context are the key determinants, and they therefore also represent the key levers you can use to shape behavior.

3 DRIVERS OF BEHAVIOR

Goals: temporary or hard wired
Memories: past experiences
Context: the environment the consumer is in, the options it allows for, the limitations it imposes

Illustration 1: Drivers of Behavior

In the next three chapters I will explore these three key drivers of behavior – memory, goals and context – and how you can shape consumer behavior by influencing them.

1 Memories

Memories are essential building blocks when it comes to making a brand choice. It is important to recognize that here I am not just talking about memories the consumer can retrieve, but all memories that have been stored in the consumer's mind. Even memories that cannot be consciously retrieved, either temporarily or permanently, can have an impact on how the consumer feels about a brand. It follows that market research studies using aided or unaided recall are essentially a waste of time.

Marketers know, of course, that memories are important, and try to get the consumer's mind to place their messages and other exposures and experiences into memory so they can influence future brand choices in favor of their brand.

Memories are not stored in isolation but are connected to other memories, and these connections are made by the nonconscious mind on the basis of how 'meaningful' they are. I have put 'meaningful' in quotation marks because the nonconscious mind cannot use rational thought or logic to work out what makes sense. Rather, it looks for some clue to indicate that particular memories are related to each other. One such clue is temporal adjacency, i.e., the simultaneous occurrence of different exposures. For example, when a consumer sees an ad that shows a brand and suggests certain qualities, it is likely that the brand memory will be connected with these qualities simply because they appeared together.

There is a simple test you can do when considering an advertising concept or idea: simply put on paper the different messages this ad would send and how these messages are interlinked. If your ad is likely to create a rich memory pattern this exercise should result in a highly integrated eco-system of messages, as shown in the following example for a fruit juice television commercial.

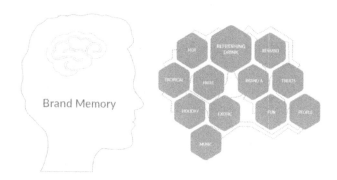

Illustration 2: *Brand Memory Pattern*

It is important to recognize, however, that the power of the message eco-system can also work against you. For example, when messages are already strongly linked with a competing brand (or any other brand, not necessarily in the same category) the consumer's nonconscious may connect your ad with that brand. Such cases of misattribution are not uncommon and may lead to your ads boosting the market share of your competitors.

This is why it is important to understand the territory that is already owned by different brands in the consumer's mind. There is a research methodology that allows you to gain such insights, called the Response Time Test (RTT). I will cover the RTT in some detail in a later section.

Codes: strong connections between memory patterns

It's not just a matter of an attribute or quality being associated with your brand, but how strong this connection is. Quite often, specific attributes are connected with several brands, but more strongly with some than with others. Less often we see a case where a brand has an absolutely dominant connection with an attribute. In these cases we could say the brand 'owns the territory' in the consumer's mind. Such dominant connections are called 'codes'.

In the world of brands there are only a few that have developed such strong connections in the minds of many consumers by consistently associating themselves with particular qualities. For example, in many markets the Disney brand is associated with family entertainment, Apple with innovation and Michelin with safety. These are brand codes, i.e., very strong connections between a brand and a quality or offer that has been built through a large number of consistent exposures.

Whenever a memory is called up it becomes stronger because the connections between the neurons making up this memory are strengthened. As the Canadian neuropsychologist Donald Hebbes famously stated way back in 1949, "neurons that fire together, wire together". When a particular attribute and a brand are frequently and consistently called up together through advertising, personal experience or other means, a strong connection develops that will eventually become so dominant that calling up one will automatically activate the other.

'Training' the brain to strongly connect two or more memory patterns is, of course, not limited to brands. For example, if somebody you meet holds out their hand you will automatically shake it without thinking about your response (replace the handshake with whatever is common in your culture). This is something you have learned and, by repeating it again and again, habitualized.

A brand that has developed a brand code in the consumer's mind will be activated whenever that code is activated. For example, when thinking about 'safety' Michelin immediately comes to mind. This is important: for most brands, their brand memory is not activated by thinking about an attribute, quality or capability. Rather, the consumer has to think of the brand first, and this is followed by the activation of some associated memories. With a brand code, on the other hand, it works in both directions: when the brand memory is activated the brand code is also activated, immediately linking the brand with a purpose, quality or capability and, importantly, when the brand code is activated the brand is immediately activated as well.

But there is more to codes than just a strong association of certain qualities with a brand. Codes often also have an influence on how we perceive contexts. For example, if a particular media channel is consistently aligned with our own views of the world we will develop a very strong association between this media channel and the qualities of being 'reliable' or 'trustworthy', and this will have an impact on how we are affected by an ad or brand story delivered by this channel rather than another.

It follows that codes are a key issue for any marketer, as the consumer's codes determine how receptive they are to your marketing messages and how these messages are interpreted. If your message is not on-code you are likely to find that the signals you send are discarded or, if they are processed by the consumer's mind, they will lead to a confused brand image that does not make it clear which goals your brand can effectively address.

Codes are not limited to the level of individual brands. Consumers also may develop some category-level codes which are important for two reasons. First, they can dominate the views the consumer has with respect to your brand. For example, if a consumer associates banks with being self-centered rather than consumer-focused, this will impact on how they see all bank brands. Secondly, they can lead to consumers rejecting whole categories, which is a problem if your brand belongs to such a category. For example, some consumers will not undertake a cruise holiday because their code for cruises is 'old people'. Even if this code is not based on facts it will influence their choice and, given this code, they are unlikely to try a cruise.

At the same time it is possible for a brand that is clearly differentiated and diametrically different to a negative category code to attract consumers; for example, a bank that is extremely consumer friendly and *can prove it with tangible actions and elements of its offer.* But it is difficult for such a brand to be heard because the category code in the consumer's mind has such a strong influence. Communications that are contrary to an existing code are typically ignored or discounted. I will explore some ways of dealing with this challenge in a later section. At this stage I simply note that category and brand codes are important – if they exist they need to be understood and taken into account when developing a brand strategy.

I am not suggesting that codes determine consumer behavior but they do determine the likelihood of a consumer:
- seeing your product as having the potential to satisfy a goal
- creating a memory of an exposure to your touchpoint
- becoming aware of your marketing communications or your product off- or on-line.

Illustration: McDonald's brand code
When McDonald's introduced healthy meal options to their menus they experienced a boost in patronage, but the vast majority of customers ended up choosing a hamburger rather than one of the new healthier options. What happened?

Many adults were introduced to fast food/hamburgers at an early age and, almost invariably, as a special treat. Fast food was a reward, a celebration, and it is no surprise that McDonald's actively encourages this by offering special birthday parties for children and including toys with children's meals.

Here is what happens when you visit McDonald's as an adult with the intention of choosing a healthy meal option, but suddenly find yourself wolfing down a hamburger:

When you visit your neighborhood McDonald's your conscious mind (your frontal lobes) decides that you will order a salad because it is good for you. But by the time you arrive at the counter to place your order, your brain has already activated your learned code that your usual fare of hamburgers will reward you and thus trigger a dopamine release. You almost automatically order your hamburger, fries and soda. In fact, research has also shown that the majority of patrons only look at the menu board *after* placing their order. In any case your nonconscious mind wins and you get to enjoy a hamburger instead of the salad your conscious mind 'knows' is the healthier option.

Sensory codes
Sensory codes are important because products and brands send sensory signals. Like other codes sensory codes are learned, many of them during childhood.

Consumers may have learned to associate soft surfaces with something positive and likeable, while hard surfaces may be linked with authority and determination. Warmth may be linked with relaxing, while cold may create tension. Sweet may be interpreted as a reward, while spicy might be linked with adulthood or sophistication (depending, of course, on the cultural context).

Because sensory codes are learned, it is possible for brands to develop new codes in the consumer's mind.

For example, in many markets it is common to use light-colored packaging for 'light' product variants, i.e., products that contain less of something that may be seen as 'bad for you', such as fat or sugar. Eventually, a code develops that leads the consumer to automatically associate lighter colored packaging in food products with a 'reduced' or 'better for you' product. Once the code is established marketers can use it to create certain perceptions. Low-tar cigarettes, for example, often use lighter colored packaging to trigger this code.

Action, cultural and behavioral codes
I mentioned earlier that you are likely to shake a hand that is held out to you when meeting a person. However, this will only happen if you grew up or live in a culture where hand-shaking is a standard greeting ritual. Just like product, brand and sensory codes, such action and

behavioral codes are learned. We develop a dress code to cover various situations, a restaurant code, a movie code (turn off your mobile phone, don't talk during the film) and so forth. The phone rings, you pick it up. A woman steps towards a door, you open it (at least you do if you are part of an older age cohort).

Some of the friction between generations is due to differences in the codes they have learned. Similarly, some of the friction between cultures is based on differences in the codes these cultures have created.

Why are action codes important?

Obviously, they are significant when creating stories that are supposed to benefit your brand, such as a television commercial or a viral campaign. But they are also relevant when it comes to product innovation and, generally, to design. I have recently been involved in a project to develop a new type of online service in a virtual world. We found that consumers judged their experience in this online world very much on the basis of how closely the navigation tool corresponded with the behavioral code they had developed playing online games.

How products are used and even the opening of product packaging can be a key element in positioning the product or brand in the consumer's mind. We know from medical research that there are two parallel paths in the brain: a sensory path that establishes what a product is, and a path that deals with motor activity and establishes what we can do with it. Importantly, our brain doesn't wait until we actually handle a product to get moving. fMRI studies have shown that our brain activates the areas responsible for picking up a bottle when we are merely shown a bottle. It follows that the brain is very much evaluating products on the basis of how to physically deal with them, even if we are not aware of this process.

Codes shape categorization and trade-off decisions
Negative categorizations present formidable marketing

challenges for brands.

Consider that the brain does not categorize inputs according to total impressions, but rather selects the key elements of an exposure to determine which category it belongs to. This applies to just about everything we experience. We learn to categorize animals despite their often vast variety in size and shape, we categorize groups of people (gender, race, how they present themselves, et cetera), places, occasions, and much more.

This leads to generalizations such as *'supermarket shopping is boring', 'banks are ripping you off'* or *'the arts are not for me'*. It is important for marketers to understand how an offer, product or brand has been classified in the consumer's mind and to attempt to change this classification if it has an unfavorable impact on sales. Here are a couple of illustrations:

Illustration: Cultural code – Wine

French parents typically encourage their children to taste wine from an early age. They often have some wine with dinner and offer their children a taste, at the same time explaining how this particular wine complements the meal. Depending on their own level of interest they may also provide some details on the history of the wine or winery, or the appellation district. And they encourage questions and discussion.

So, as French children grow up, the learned code for wine becomes *'an elevated dining (or consumption) experience'*. Even when they enter adulthood and start going out with their peers or partners, they rarely get blind drunk. More likely, they order interesting wines and discuss their qualities. They enjoy the consumption of the wine rather than the experience of being drunk.

There are, however, many countries where parents don't introduce their children to wine from an early age. Rather, they portray wine (and alcohol in general) as something forbidden, for adults only, with a focus on the potential negative outcome of drinking alcohol (intoxication) rather than the process of consuming and appreciating it.

Of course, children become aware through movies and television shows, if not through observation in the real world, of people being drunk and possibly doing silly things. So the learned code for wine becomes *'forbidden, desirable, exciting'* and as soon as they can get (legal or illegal) access to alcohol they experiment and, sooner or later, get truly tanked.

This illustrates how cultural codes classify a whole category and – like any other codes – shape the meaning of products, brands, activities and situations which in turn shape perceptions, attitudes and behavior.

Illustration: Cultural code – Performing arts
Learned codes determine to a great extent how inclined consumers are to buy a ticket to attend a live arts performance.

In many countries governments attempt to encourage participation by introducing young people to the arts. Typically, this is done as part of a school program. I will use two examples to illustrate how the design of such a school program impacts on the development of a code for the performing arts, which in turn has a determining impact on audience attendance figures.

In Australia, school programs are typically designed as an organized excursion to a special school matinee. School students are taken by teachers to a theater to attend a performance. They often read relevant material before the event or have some discussions in class. After the performance they may be quizzed on various aspects of the play, testing their understanding and providing the teacher with an opportunity to fill in any gaps.

In Austria, the Viennese state government has designed a program called Theater der Jugend (translated, '*Theater for Youth*'). One day someone turns up in the classroom during a break and tells the students that they can attend a free performance by simply taking one of the tickets that person leaves behind.

Naturally, students organize themselves into groups of friends, who pick up a ticket each to take advantage of this opportunity. The performance is not a special school matinee, but a regular evening performance. One of the advantages the students see is that they are likely to get their parents' permission to go out, as this is obviously a sanctioned program. So they go out in small groups, have the odd forbidden cigarette or drink, and enjoy the play in the company of their friends.

So much for background. The question is: what will the learned code for the (performing) arts be in these two countries, given the very different introduction to the audience experience?

Not surprisingly, in countries such as Australia the learned code is typically around *'educational, school, imposed'* and an average of 50% of all seats in performing arts centers stay empty, with young people generally not interested in attending performances. In Vienna, meanwhile, the learned code is more likely to be *'great night out with friends'* allowing the arts to find a natural place in the repertoire of entertainment choices and, not surprisingly, the theaters are filled with an audience that spans all age groups.

Clearly, the learned category code for the (performing) arts has a significant impact on consumer behavior.

2 Goals

Goals determine what the consumer is looking for when making a purchase decision. When a goal is activated consumers typically draw on their memories to identify how that goal was successfully addressed in the past, or which new options may look promising. As I will explain in the next section, context can also play a role by suggesting certain ways of addressing a goal. All this happens in the nonconscious mind. While the consumer may also consciously explore options, these considerations are very much shaped by the input the nonconscious mind delivers.

It may be helpful to start by clarifying what goals are, and what they are not.

Needs do not drive brand choice
While marketers often use the terms 'needs' and 'goals' interchangeably when talking about drivers of brand choice, the two are actually very different from each other.

Stated needs are simply rationalizations. Consumers are not sure why they buy what they buy, as they cannot access the nonconscious part of their brain that drives their brand choices. They are left to rationalize, i.e., to interpret their choice in a way that 'makes sense'. However the nonconscious mind does not make what we would consider logical, rational decisions. Rather, it looks for indicators, clues that may suggest that a goal can be satisfied by an available option.

Later in this book I will explore how you can prime consumers to select your offer above competitive options by using simple, low key signals and exposures the consumer is typically not even aware of. Priming, which often solicits irrational but predictable behavior, is a great illustration of how consumers are not aware of the goals that drive their brand choice. Indeed, the effectiveness of priming is evidence that stated needs simply miss the target.

Emotions do not drive brand choice
We know that the more richly an event is categorized by the emotions surrounding it, the longer it will be remembered and the more detailed that memory will be. We also know that decisions require emotional involvement. Accident victims who have damage to the emotional center of their brain can have a perfectly normal discussion with you, but they can't make even the simplest decision. All decisions require emotions.

However, while emotions are essential to any purchase decision, they are not the *drivers* behind these decisions.

Let me illustrate this by using a simple example: I offer you an ice cream. How are you going to react?
- If you have never had ice cream before you are unlikely to get a dopamine hit, as your nonconscious mind cannot see how ice cream can address a goal because there are no memories suggesting that it could. (For the sake of simplicity I have ignored other goals, such as to seek out new experiences).
- If you don't like ice cream your nonconscious mind will again fail to see that my offer allows you to address a goal, so you will reject it without having experienced a pleasing dopamine release.
- If you like ice cream but have just eaten a bucket of it you would have already addressed your goal and you won't get a dopamine hit when faced with more of the same.
- Finally, if you love ice cream your nonconscious mind will see it as addressing a goal. As a result, you will get a dopamine hit that makes you feel good as you accept the ice cream I have so generously offered you - and you get another dopamine release when you enjoy the consumption experience.

The difference between these scenarios lies in the *goals* that are active in your (nonconscious) mind. The same offer will trigger a dopamine hit when it addresses a goal, but not when it doesn't. The goal is the key driver of the purchase. The sequence is as follows: *When you address a goal you get a dopamine release. The dopamine hit makes you feel good, i.e., you experience an emotional response.* It follows that the emotion is a result – rather than a driver – of your behavior.

You could argue that we can measure emotions as a safe indicator of a goal having been addressed. Unfortunately such a measure could be highly misleading as it may not be clear at all what is triggering these emotions. Consider an advertisement that triggers emotion. Are the emotions the result of the ad addressing a goal that is related to the brand, or have they been triggered by some other aspect of the ad such as the talent, the music, or even a promise or commitment that is not related to the brand? Coming back to my ice cream example, you might get a dopamine hit when the love of your life offers you an ice cream even if you don't enjoy ice cream at all.

An often quoted example is the Pepsi Refresh Project, an outstanding case of what can happen when a brand – using its own marketing resources, aided and abetted by social media – successfully taps into the growing desire of people to do something constructive.[2]

Pepsi offered to donate $20 million to a range of causes. Consumers were encouraged to put forward worthy causes and to vote for them, with Pepsi allocating grants ranging from $5,000 to $250,000 to the causes that received the most votes.

Some 80 million votes were cast – a great success from a social engagement perspective – and Pepsi awarded more than $20 million to some 1,000 projects. Forbes magazine called it one of the year's best social media campaigns. The project was featured in thousands of

---

[2] For more detail see Scott Goodson, *Uprising. How to build a brand and change the world by sparking cultural movements*, McGraw Hill 2012

local newspapers and television stories, mostly praising Pepsi for creating an innovative social media program. However, while Pepsi's campaign attracted some 80,000,000 votes, the brand lost market share: the campaign did not have a positive impact on sales.

From a neuromarketing perspective this is not surprising. Putting up a cause you feel strongly about and hoping for a grant triggers a dopamine release (and emotions), as does voting for causes you believe in. But you are addressing goals that are not linked to the brand. Sure, the brand is a facilitator, but it does not play an essential role in this program. The ads and other collateral presenting the proposition for this campaign would have tested extremely well in consumer research by generating a high level of emotions, but this measure would have been totally misleading.

Temporary versus permanent goals

A dopamine release is triggered whenever a temporary or a (somewhat) permanent goal is addressed. So does it matter which it is? If we only consider the end result - the dopamine hit - it doesn't matter. But when it comes to your brand strategy you will find that it is generally more cost-effective and safer to address a more permanent, hard-wired goal. One of the immediate advantages is that you don't need to undertake any market research because these goals are biological in nature, i.e., there is scientific evidence that they exist.

Temporary goals are goals such as hunger, which manifest themselves when the nonconscious mind decides that something is needed to avoid a physical or mental deficiency. Once it has been addressed, the goal is de-activated.

Permanent goals, which I call *Deep Rooted Drivers of Behavior (DRDs)*, are hard-wired brain circuits that drive behavior over longer periods of time – sometimes a whole lifetime - and are common to many people.

Let me use the ***Male and Female DRDs*** as an example: All of us are female for the first eight weeks after conception. Around that time, something happens if our genes carry a Y chromosome: testosterone floods the brain and creates unique circuits that drive male behavior while another hormone, MIS, destroys the brain circuits that drive female behavior. If, on the other hand, our genes have two X chromosomes we are destined to remain female.

These male and female brain circuits have a huge impact on how individuals interpret the world around them, how they feel about what they experience, and what importance they attach to different experiences.

Women end up with higher levels of estrogen, progesterone and oxytocin, as well as a thicker corpus callosum which allows them to concurrently access the emotional and rational sides of their brain more successfully than men. They have advantages when it comes to:
- communication
- gut feelings
- reading others' emotions
- social nuances
- nurturing skills
- anger suppression.

Men have higher levels of testosterone and MIS and tend to perform better with respect to:
- exploratory behavior
- muscular and motor control
- spatial skills
- rough play
- focus on self
- sexual pursuit.

The important point is that men and women are not the same – they each have particular advantages compared to the other gender. Arguably, women have the more valuable set of advantages, but the main point from the marketing perspective is that they are different.

Or consider the ***MotherhoodDRD***. Progesterone, estrogen and oxytocin create brain circuits that have some permanency. These new brain circuits are likely to be weakened or destroyed during menopause, but will drive behavior until then.

Another universal DRD is the *BelongingDRD*. We are hardwired to belong because anyone who lived in isolation in a hostile natural environment – where humankind spent the vast majority of time during our evolution – had a very short life expectancy. It is worth noting that Belonging is a stronger driver in women than in men. This is because women had to build informal networks with other women to fight off the physically stronger men who would have happily killed infants who had other fathers, seeking to ensure their own genes were carried forward into the next generation instead.

The *CompetitionDRD* is a stronger driver in men. A simple way of activating the CompetitionDRD is to create opposition or an enemy. For example, setting up Apple as the opposite or enemy of PCs activates the 'us and them' feeling that is driven by the CompetitionDRD.

We are all hardwired to explore – the *ExplorationDRD* – although this is typically a stronger driver in males than females.

Dopamine ensures that we all seek rewards. The *RewardDRD* is probably the most obvious but there are of course many different ways of rewarding consumers. The essential point is that you need to trigger a dopamine release that makes the person feel good – and then seek more and even stronger rewards once their dopamine level declines.

There are also DRDs that are particularly relevant to the execution of marketing communications, such as the *EmpathyDRD* and *ShortcutDRD*.

The *EmpathyDRD* is, strictly speaking, not a brain circuit but rather comprises of a different type of neuron that can flood the brain with emotions. These mirror neurons allow us to feel the emotions that others are feeling. Mirror neurons are the reason we respond emotionally when watching a movie or reading a well-told story. They will also boost the feelings we share with a group;

for example, barracking for our team during a sporting match is much more emotionally involving when we do it together with like-minded people as we can feel their emotions, which lifts the intensity of our own.

I have left one of the most important DRDs until last: the ***ShortcutDRD*** that drives us to, well, seek shortcuts. Why is this the case?

In the past I have myself used the argument that the brain represents only 2 to 3 percent of our body weight, yet uses some 20 percent of our energy. Thinking less is therefore a highly effective way of saving energy. This sounds like a pretty compelling argument – but it is not right.

For some 4 million years humans did not have a conscious mind. They did not have frontal lobes that allowed them to analyze, plan and generally think about options, evaluate these options and make decisions. They only had their nonconscious mind at their disposal. And, being unable to consciously think, the nonconscious mind had to identify those indicators that would suggest a positive outcome and then act on them. Not surprisingly, this approach has been hardwired over time and, given that the nonconscious mind is faster than the conscious mind, it does influence the way we make choices by using indicators that eliminate the need to consciously think.

Therefore, it was not the need to save energy that led to shortcut decisions being hardwired but rather a lack of alternatives, given that our forebears did not have a conscious mind that allowed them to analyze, explore and rationalize. Today, the ***ShortcutDRD*** is very much alive and at work. While we now have a 'new brain' that can analyze and make rational comparisons and evaluations, it is no match for the nonconscious mind that is faster and more powerful, and able to find shortcuts that eliminate a (heavy) involvement of the conscious mind.

One point is clear: marketing campaigns are complex and

multi-layered, but well-designed initiatives that are aligned with DRDs can cut through these layers and solicit a positive response from consumers who would otherwise have bought competitor brands rather than your own.

Addressing the consumer's goals

Understanding goals is a useful first step, but unless you can translate this knowledge into action it won't make a positive impact on your brand strategy. In a later section I will introduce a research methodology you can us to identify the drivers of purchase (attributes, qualities or capabilities that are seen to address a goal) and to what extent your brand – and your competitors' brands - are associated with them.

Some of the avenues you can explore are:

Convincing the consumer that your brand can satisfy a goal it has not been seen to satisfy in the past
It is sometimes possible for marketers to convince the consumer that their goal(s) can be addressed in new ways, i.e., through their own brands, products or services.

For example, a status-seeking consumer may use their choice of car, holiday destination, clothing, briefcase, watch, pen or restaurant to satisfy their goal to express their status. Over time, marketers have added to this list by positioning brands and associated products on a status platform. In the last decade, they have already added mobile phones, computer tablets, online games and other products and services to the list. In some markets, the brand of mineral water you drink, the bakery where you get the bread for your dinner party, and even where you park your car have become a means of expressing status.

The consumer's relationship with brands is based on the extent to which a brand is seen as a way to satisfy their goals. These are all examples of marketers finding new ways of addressing consumers' goals through brand and product positioning. However it is difficult, if not impossible, for a brand to create new goals in the consumer's mind. It is more realistic to try to convince the consumer that a brand can satisfy their existing goals.

Claiming that your brand or product can satisfy goals that have so far been satisfied by brands and products from a different category typically requires a disruptive strategy.

Consider Dove's repositioning from a well-known but run-of-the-mill body-care brand to a brand that understands women, values natural beauty and aims to lift the self-esteem of girls. The *'Real Beauty'* campaign was a disruptive strategy that allowed Dove to offer its brand as a means of addressing goals that were poorly addressed by cosmetics and body-care brands.

Dove is also a great example for how well-defined and ingenious positioning and the associated marketing strategy won't work *unless it meets with pre-existing goals in the consumer's mind.* The Dove strategy failed in markets such as Russia and China where the consumer's goal was generally to lift their self-esteem and social status by using the latest cosmetics (or by using any cosmetics at all, if their income allowed it) rather than by celebrating natural beauty.

Timing of goal satisfaction
Neuroscience research has shown that goals get stronger if they are not satisfied immediately. This suggests that you may be better off activating a goal in the consumer's mind some time before you offer to satisfy it.

There is, however, a potential problem: the consumer might find a way to satisfy that goal in a way that does not involve the purchase of your brand! Typically goals can be satisfied in many different ways, and most often you are not only competing with other brands in your category, but also with brands in different categories and even things the consumer can do without making a purchase at all. So delayed goal satisfaction is something to be explored cautiously, but it is certainly worth considering.

Take a television ad for chocolate. This may activate the goal to be rewarded, indulge, feel comforted or special. The consumer heaves his bottom off the couch and wanders into the kitchen where he finds a tub of ice cream in the freezer - which satisfies the very same goals.

Or consider a simple in-store taste testing. Let's take the example of a brand that offers mothers an opportunity to give their children something that makes them happy and active, such as a healthy breakfast food.

You could activate this goal at the entrance to the supermarket by displaying happy children being active outdoors, enjoying life. You would not present your product or brand at this point, but simply focus on imagery that activates the shopper's goal to have happy, healthy children. This is because you don't want to encourage the shopper's mind to put up counter-arguments, which may arise when they see which brand is promoting these benefits.

Further into the reaches of the supermarket you would position a taste test, where you would again display the images of happy children, but this time linked with your brand. Importantly, the staff conducting the taste test would prattle on about happy children and how important it is to give children a breakfast they enjoy and that nourishes them, because happy children are children that are active and explore their world, and so on, and so on.

Assuming you have activated the right goal at the store entrance shoppers are more likely to participate in the taste test, to enjoy the experience, and to buy - because this is an opportunity to satisfy the nonconscious goal you have activated.

However, the risk is that the shopper comes across another brand or product that would satisfy the very same goal before their journey takes them to your taste test.

Goals are pretty stable, but they may be addressed in new ways

While DRDs drive fundamental consumer behavior by encouraging them to address specific goals, there is often a difference in how goals are addressed as people age. The key neurotransmitters change when aging. I will use males as an example here as there are disruptive events (pregnancy, motherhood, menopause) that make the patterns in women less straightforward.

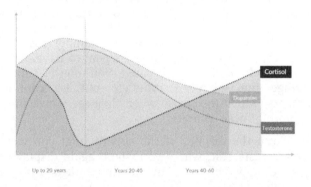

Illustration 3: changes in neurotransmitters in males due to ageing

As the graph clearly shows, men reach the peak of their testosterone and dopamine release during their early twenties, with the level declining slowly during their remaining lifetime. Meanwhile cortisol, also called the 'worry' transmitter, increases with age.

An astute marketer can translate this into specific, age-related behavioral patterns to guide *execution* when using communications channels that reach particular age groups. Let's assume a consumer is an adventurer and loves the excitement that adventures bring. As this person ages he is likely to change the way excitement is delivered. While earlier in his life he may have sought risky new experiences, he is likely to change to less risky adventures as he reaches middle age. As he gets older still he is likely to seek repeat experiences rather than new ones, as his high cortisol level discourages him from experiences that are completely unfamiliar.

In summary, goal activation is hugely important because it leads to sales. Every campaign, engagement opportunity, social media initiative, package design – in fact, every key touchpoint – should be designed with goal activation and satisfaction in mind.

3 Context

Memories are historical in nature but there are almost always some current contextual factors that may impact on the purchase decision, such as new inputs (e.g., shopper marketing initiatives or input from a sales assistant) or restrictions that impact on how goals could be addressed (e.g., a limited range of options, or affordability). These and other environmental factors constitute the context within which the consumer makes the purchase decision.

Remember that the nonconscious mind is constantly looking for indictors that may help it interpret and classify sensory inputs. This means that when a consumer is exposed to an ad the nonconscious mind will process not just the ad, but also any other contextual elements such as the media the ad is delivered by. For example, there may be memories classifying a particular news site as 'unreliable' while another site has been classified as 'trustworthy'. The same ad appearing in one or the other will have a very different impact on how the message is processed and stored in memory.

Marketers know, of course, that context is important. This is why they create environments with particular features and qualities reflected in the design of supermarkets, showrooms, bank branches, offices, and so forth. Even product packaging can have a significant impact on the way the product and its brand are processed.

But the importance of context goes a lot further. Once a brand or product has been classified the nonconscious mind is likely to pick up messages that are aligned with this classification. Take the current US President, Donald Trump, as an example: if you have classified Trump as a great President you will be more aware of any positive news or messages and you will also interpret news in a positive way. If you have classified him as a President who does not live up to acceptable standards you will do just the opposite.

You can develop contexts that favor your brand. Imagine you are driving along a country road past a sign announcing that a McDonald's can be found in the next town. Regardless of whether you are consciously aware of the sign when you pass it, the sign can still activate the goal to indulge in a burger and thus increase the likelihood of you stopping at the fast food outlet.

A lemon scent in a restaurant will lead to an increase in seafood orders – but only in countries where seafood is typically served with a slice of lemon. The smell of lemon activates the nonconscious goal to enjoy a delicious seafood dish. Needless to say, this would not happen with consumers who hate seafood, as seafood would not address any of their goals.

Of course, the sign and the lemon scent are part of the context within which decisions are being made. Creating context that send *signals* to the brain that trigger a goal or suggest a particular way of addressing a goal is called *priming*, and priming is one of the most essential marketing tools.

Sending the right signals

The consumer's nonconscious mind cannot understand analytical concepts. It seeks out even small signals to make sense of an exposure's meaning, allowing it to decide if a memory should be created and, if so, which other memories it should be linked with. This means that signals are a key determinant of meaning, and as a marketer you have an opportunity to create signals that will suggest your brand has certain qualities or capabilities, can address certain goals, or even encourage the consumer to make a purchase right there and then.

Your nonconscious mind is always looking for meaningful signals. The difficulty is that the brain receives an abundance of signals, and your signals are less likely to be stored in the consumer's memory if they are not related to a goal.

Look through a magazine and you may not 'see' any of

the washing machine ads. Not even one. A few weeks later your washing machine breaks down and you consider replacing it. Look through a magazine and you suddenly see every washing machine ad – even if you hadn't set out to look for them. The context has changed and your mind has registered that a washing machine could address one of your goals, so washing machine ads have suddenly become relevant.

This means that you need to take care to ensure every signal you send:
- is on-code with respect to your product offer, i.e., *relevance*
- consistently reflects the brand's positioning, i.e., *contributes to creating a brand code* (I will present a simple way of achieving this by using brand vision archetypes in a later section)
- creates a distinct and credible impression, i.e., *effective differentiation.*

If the signals you send are not on-code, there is a significant risk that the consumer will simply ignore your signals. There is also the risk that signals which are not in tune with your desired brand positioning will confuse the consumer.

The vast majority of marketers underestimate the importance of the signals they send. I did so as well. At the time, it seemed rather silly that what seemed only a minor signal could have so much impact, but I have since been convinced by scientific research that demonstrates that even the most marginal signals can have a profound impact on perceptions, attitudes and behavior.

Here are a few examples[3]:

- At Yale University, participants in an experiment were asked to interview a hypothetical job applicant and decide whether they would offer that person a job or not. Group 1 got a cold drink before they interviewed the person, and Group 2 a hot drink. You may have guessed it: Group 2 made far more positive judgments than Group 1.
- In a University of Groningen study, money in an unmarked envelope was put into mail boxes, arranged in a way that allowed anyone approaching the letter box to see the envelope and the money in it. Observers noted how many people took the money and put it into their pocket. The results showed that this happened significantly more often when the mail box was dirty and defaced with graffiti then when the money was in a clean mail box.
- The underlying principle that the environment primes behavior was borne out in a large-scale experiment when the New York police achieved a significant reduction in *serious* crime by focusing on *petty* crime and misdemeanors, cleaning up the underground system, reducing graffiti, and so forth.
- Meanwhile, at Duke University, participants were placed in front of a monitor and asked to carry out a series of tasks such as analyzing pictures and adding up numbers. Two logos – IBM and Apple – were shown so briefly that they were not consciously recognized (this was confirmed after the session when participants were asked if they saw any logos). Participants were then asked to carry out a creativity test, such as finding as many uses for a brick as

---

[3] I have collected these from various sources including Stephen J. Genco, Andrew P. Pohlmann, Peter Steidl, Neuromarketing for Dummies, Wiley 2013; Scheier, Christian and Dirk Held, *Wie Werbung Wirkt. Erkenntnisse des Neuromarketing*, Haufe 2010; Scheier Christian, Dirk Bayas- Linke and Johannes Schneider, *Codes. Die geheime Sprache der Produkte*, Haufe 2010; A.K. Pradeep, *The Buying Brain. Secrets for selling to the subconscious mind*, Wiley 2010.

possible. Those who had been exposed to the Apple logo had far more ideas than those exposed to the IBM logo, and an independent jury that didn't know where the ideas came from judged the Apple group's ideas as better.
- At the University of Michigan, an experiment was carried out using restaurant menus. When menus were easy to read and presented using an everyday font, the food was expected to be simple. When the same menu was presented in a hard-to-read but exclusive-looking font, the meals were expected to be complex and made using an elevated cooking style.
- The same happened with fitness routines. When a simple font was used to describe a fitness routine, it was estimated that it would take 8.2 minutes. With a hard-to-read font, estimates went up to an average of 15.1 minutes.

Essentially, this means that your mind picks up even small details and assigns meaning to them. When a signal indicates to the consumer that a particular offer will allow them to realize a goal more effectively than would other offers or means, the consumer buys.

But the nonconscious mind is extremely sensitive to signals, and an exposure is not likely to be successful if most of the signals it sends are on-code but others aren't. Marlboro offers a great case example: In 1962 their advertising agency developed a successful campaign, the Marlboro Cowboy. Sales went through the roof! The client and the agency felt they had finally solved the problem of poor sales: it was simply a matter of rolling out more 'Marlboro Cowboy' campaigns.

Despite their best efforts, however, they saw the next eight Marlboro Cowboy campaigns, spanning the years from 1963 to 1966, fail. The reason was that some of the signals were not representative of the cowboy image American consumers had in their minds: they were off-code. This may include such subtle errors as showing a cowboy in an urban setting or a group of cowboys sitting under a tree relaxing. Finally, in 1966 the agency cracked the code for 'cowboy' and the subsequent campaigns were a great success, until advertising cigarettes was prohibited by law in 1972.

Tropicana orange juice provides a more recent, but by no means less spectacular, example. A change in package design led to a loss of 30 million Euros in sales within just a couple of months, with Tropicana destined to move from its number one position in many markets to becoming an irrelevant brand. Management reverted to the old package design to avoid this fate.

Clearly, package recognition would have been a major contributor to this disaster. (I will discuss later how habitual buying relies on an *alert trigger*, i.e., the familiar package that is automatically picked up.) But it has also been convincingly argued that the new package did not send the right signals: freshness - symbolized in the old packaging by showing a straw sticking out of an orange - had been replaced by a fancy glass that few people would even use. The package was completely off-code.

Goals are the drivers of the purchase. The signals must activate one or more goals and/or suggest that the offer will address them. The codes work in your favor when you have developed a brand or product code in the consumer's mind that recognizes your offer as relevant (again, judging by the signals you send), or they can work against you when you send signals that are in conflict with the code.

The part of the brain that processes a signal determines how the signal is interpreted, mainly based on past experiences that have been stored and which serve as reference points. However, this part of the brain – the nonconscious mind - does not use logic. It simply uses the available references to classify. This is why, when a font in an exclusive-looking style is used, the brain concludes that the offer is exclusive (as long as other signals don't deliver evidence to the contrary). Or, when a brand activates the 'creativity' brand code, the brain activates an extensive neural network associated with creativity, which in fact may lift the person's creative ability.

In summary, the signals you send through your packaging, branding, product features, marketing communications, choice of distribution channels, social media, point-of-sale promotions, brand activation and other initiatives are all vital to your success. The colors, fonts, layout, and just about any other detail you use in representing your brand – including the choice of people you use to represent you, their facial expressions, body language, the words used, pauses in delivery – are all critical to maximizing the positive impact of your marketing initiatives.

4 A roadmap of the consumer's mind

Let me bring together the key elements we have just covered in a roadmap. Dopamine drives the consumer to act, but brand choice is influenced by a number of important factors as shown in the following flow-chart.

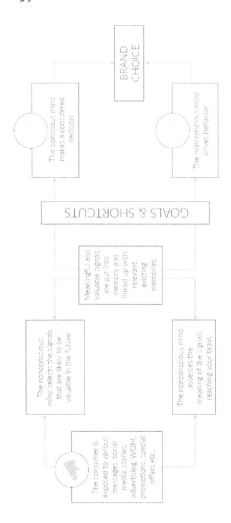

The sequence of events is as follows:

When the consumer is exposed to your brand – via packaging, an ad, social media comments, or any other touchpoint – the nonconscious mind will decide if this exposure is worth placing into memory. If it is, the nonconscious mind will also decide if this new memory is to be linked with other, existing memories. It may also alert the consumer to the exposure, i.e., activate the conscious mind, which means the consumer is thinking about the exposure – but this is the exception rather than the rule. In many markets consumers are exposed to thousands of ads each day, yet they are only consciously aware of a small percentage of these. It follows that many exposures are processed by the nonconscious without the consumer ever becoming aware of them.

The consumer's brand choice will be shaped by these memories, which will also impact on how the consumer reacts to two key factors influencing brand choice: goals and context. The consumer will seek to address one or more goals, and their memories may suggest an effective way of doing this.

Similarly, memories are likely to influence how contexts are interpreted.

The brand choice may be driven entirely by the non-conscious mind (e.g., a habitual repeat purchase, where the consumer picks up a grocery product without giving it any attention) or the conscious mind may get involved. But even in the latter case, it is clear that the way the consumer develops preferences and feels about various brands has been shaped largely by the nonconscious mind through memories, goals and the interpretation of context.

In summary, the sequence '*goals – memories – context*' is a reasonable way to describe how the consumer's mind makes purchase decisions. However, the situation is a lot more complex because of interactions between these three elements. Goals can be triggered by memories and contexts; contexts can create new memories; and goals can determine contexts (such as by driving the consumer to particular options like buying online versus visiting a particular retail outlet).

5 Habitual buying: driven by memories

Too often we assume that consumers who regularly buy the same brand have a strong brand preference. However, most likely these consumers are simply engaging in habitual buying. They aren't making purchase decisions but are simply repeating a behavior without giving it a second thought. This behavior is driven by their memories, i.e., by their nonconscious mind, without any conscious intervention. I could have covered habitual buying in the section on memories but it is such an important issue that I decided to give it its own chapter.

Think for a moment about your own day-to-day activities. You are on autopilot when carrying out routine tasks such as brushing your teeth, having a shower, drinking your coffee, walking or driving to work, switching on your computer, eating your sandwich at lunch, and so forth. A US study estimated that we are on autopilot for approximately 45 percent of our waking time, typically doing the same things in the same contexts. Thus, habitual behavior is very common and it should come as no surprise that is also very common when it comes to making purchases.

Marketers often assume that consumers actively make purchase decisions when they buy a product or service, especially when the product or service in question is one they are responsible for. The truth is that consumers make many of their regular purchases habitually. The original purchase decision that provides the foundation for this habitual buying behavior may have been made many years ago. This phenomenon has been studied extensively, especially in the FMCG category. Ehrenberg, the father of consumer panels, has proven again and again that repeat purchases are typically not a result of brand loyalty but of habit.

True loyalty is based on consumers believing that the

brand they buy is the best choice for them.[4] Habitual buying means that the consumer doesn't think about whether the product or brand is the *best* choice for them; they simply repeat past purchases. This suggests that the brand 'works' for them, but we cannot assume that they are loyal to it.

Habitual buying allows consumers to simplify their lives by avoiding the need to spend many hours checking all options open to them with each purchase. You may recall the ShortcutDRD. Habitual buying is arguably the greatest achievement of this DRD because it offers processing fluency - there is not a single step in this process that requires thinking. Here are some typical habitual buying situations:

Many FMCG purchases are habitual in nature. When buying groceries in a supermarket many consumers habitually buy the same brand without making a conscious purchase decision.

Some shopper marketing experts claim that 95% of purchase decisions are made in-store. This is an incomplete assessment of the situation. The truth is more likely that approximately 95% of grocery items are *bought habitually*. The purchase decision for the remaining 5% of purchases is typically made in-store. However, the consumer was most likely primed long before they entered the store, with advertising, promotions, word-of-mouth and past experience all playing an important role in their decision. I am not suggesting that shopper marketing is not important or effective, but its strength lies in its ability to turn a habitual purchase into a considered one, leading to the purchase of a different brand. Out-of-stock situations can also disrupt habitual buying.

Only purchases that carry a high degree of emotion – perhaps the consumer enjoys the process of shopping, or is worried about getting it wrong because it is a

---

[4] *'Best'* is defined by the particular goal they want to address and their perceptions of the brand's ability to do so.

significant purchase and they have little experience with the category – are likely to naturally follow a conscious purchase decision making process.

But habitual buying is by no means limited to FMCGs. How many consumers review which search engine they use every time they search for something online? How many review their magazine or newspaper subscriptions every time a renewal payment falls due? The same applies to Pay TV and performing arts subscriptions, memberships, insurances, superannuation, savings plans and many other types of regular payments. Consumers don't review their banking arrangements every time they make a home loan payment but simply stick with the same financial institution.

Even when the fee payable varies from period to period, consumers often habitualize. For example, they don't re-evaluate the companies who provide their household utilities every time they get an invoice. They automatically pay it.

Having said that, as a review of these service providers *can* be triggered by a bill, it is no wonder that many suppliers encourage consumers to make payments by automatic debit. This eliminates the moment when the consumer might look at a bill and think '*maybe there is a less expensive option*' or '*is this really worth that much money?*' It is also clear that more frequent, smaller payments are less likely to lead to a re-evaluation of purchases than larger, less frequent (such as yearly) payments.

Some consumers even habitualize, to some extent, the purchase of major items such as cars, electronic equipment and holidays. In the case of cars, they may habitually buy the same brand, and limit their purchase decision to the model and specifications. Similarly, Apple, Samsung or Huawei owners may consider buying the next model without ever seriously considering alternative brands.

Naturally, we can more often expect habitual purchases

with products that are bought more frequently than those that have much longer replacement cycles. For example, we are more likely to develop a mobile phone 'habit' than a sound system 'habit.'

Finally, there are habits that are not brand, product or occasion-based but that follow certain rules or heuristics. For example, a consumer may have a rule like *'don't buy unless the brand is on sale,'* or even *'don't buy at all unless there is a major sale on.'* These habits can become as entrenched as the habitual purchase of specific items. Retailers have spent considerable sums to promote such behavior and are now suffering the consequences, as many consumers have adopted heuristics that see them shopping only when retailers offer significant cost savings.

Once we stop and consider the wide range of habits that determine what consumers buy, we can see that habitual buying is actually a much more important and difficult challenge for marketers to address than is the task of influencing considered purchase decisions.

Obviously, the vast majority of habitual purchases rest on a purchase decision made at some stage in the consumer's past. It therefore makes sense to try to attract consumers entering particular product markets early on and to encourage them to develop a habitual buying behavior before another brand does.

In some product categories, physiological factors help. For example, we tend to become used to certain flavors early in our lives and these preferred flavors stick with us for a long time, often for life. Chocolate manufacturers such as Cadbury actively pursue young consumers and get them used to the distinctive Cadbury taste. Once this has happened, these consumers are likely to prefer Cadbury over, say, Hershey, and vice versa. This is apparently why Cadbury always uses top-quality chocolate in fun items aimed at children.

Let's now explore a neuroscience-based view of habitual buying to see how you can most effectively deal with the marketing challenge that habitual buying poses.

The neuroscience perspective
Habits are learned. This is why you first have to learn and gain experience before you can leave it to your nonconscious mind to take over. As a simple example think about the difference between learning to drive a car and almost automatically driving once you are an experienced driver. Learning through repetitive behavior creates memories of how to do the task. Your nonconscious mind then relies on the massive bank of memories that represent experiences you have gathered in the past.

Letting your nonconscious take care of activities is, of course, a very important part of how your brain works. If you couldn't let your nonconscious mind take over activities you have learnt, you would not be able to do more than one thing at a time because all of your conscious attention would be focused on it. To put this in perspective: your nonconscious mind can process 11 million bits of information per second, while your conscious mind is limited to 40 bits per second.

The habitual mind, being part of the nonconscious, is nonverbal so it doesn't learn by reading or by listening to an explanation. It only learns through repetition, nonconsciously associating an action with an outcome.

This explains why consumers who consciously decide to switch to another brand often fall back into their old buying habits. Their decision to make the switch has no impact on their learned behavior. If they are not in conscious mode while shopping, there is a good chance they will simply follow their old established habits. Research undertaken by Nielsen shows that customers who purchase a brand eight times have a 97% likelihood of buying the brand a ninth time. This helps explain why major brands are so dominant. It's market inertia. Customers continue to buy out of habit.

In summary, habitual buying is *learned* behavior. There is no cognitive process, no consideration of alternatives, and no assessment of benefits once the habit has been established. The purchase is driven by stimulus-response. The process has been habitualized and delegated to the nonconscious, which does not engage in cognitive thinking.

Repeat and alert triggers
But how does your nonconscious mind know which behaviors to repeat when? Why don't you find yourself sitting up in bed at night, acting as if you are driving a car? The simple answer is that there are *repeat triggers* your brain can interpret, and the habitual behavior is only demonstrated when one of these repeat triggers activates it.

When you get into your car, the familiar environment triggers driving behavior. If you have ever rented an unfamiliar car or bought a new car, you will most likely have experienced *alert triggers* caused by, for example, the unfamiliar instruments or their unfamiliar positioning on the dashboard. In these cases you have to give your conscious attention to starting and driving the car until your mind becomes familiar with its particular instruments and features, at which point your nonconscious can again take over.

In other words, there are two pre-requisites for the nonconscious mind to take over:
- First, you must have 'trained' your mind by carrying out the behavior many times before (the number of times necessary depends on how complex and variable the context is).
- Secondly, there has to be a *repeat trigger* that starts the habitual behavior, i.e., one that leads to your nonconscious taking over.

It follows that the marketer's challenge is not just to develop habitual buying, but also to create repeat triggers that activate the desired consumer behavior. In many instances the repeat trigger is simply the visual image of the packaging or the brand name.

While repeat triggers spark off the habitual behavior,

alert triggers disrupt habitual behavior and bring the conscious mind into play. Any change to a product – including features, performance, appearance, price, or channel of distribution – can be an alert trigger and move the consumer from a habitual response into a conscious mind-led review.

Establishing habits
As habits develop through repetition, it follows that you need consumers to stick with a brand or product for a period of time for the desired habits to develop. There are many strategies marketers can use to make this happen, from offering significant discounts on large volume purchases to creating challenges or trial periods that encourage the consumer to keep using the product for an extended period, to positioning the brand as part of an existing routine. To illustrate the last point, consider mouthwash. Brushing one's teeth is, for many consumers, already a habit. By linking the use of mouthwash to this activity, consumers are more likely to habitualize using mouthwash as well as toothpaste.

The most important point is that we know that consumers are likely to develop habitual purchasing behavior for the majority of frequently bought products. It is therefore important to encourage brand purchases when a consumer enters a product category.

For example, first time mothers will eventually habitually buy a wide range of baby products from nappies to creams, baby foods to soap. It therefore makes sense to present the mother with some free product samples while she is still recovering from giving birth in a maternity ward. Likewise, when consumers move into new homes they will need to establish new shopping habits. It therefore makes sense for a local supermarket, convenience store or hardware store to work with real estate agents to offer these consumers a welcome pack with special coupons for their retail outlets.

In these instances it is relatively easy to identify the

target group, and there are existing intermediaries such as companies that distribute free samples to maternity wards or real estate agents who handle property in the area.

Sometimes all a marketer can do is target specific age groups. I have already mentioned the importance of getting young consumers to develop a chocolate preference. The same applies to tea, coffee and other products, although some preferences will be shaped by what is already being bought habitually by the household the consumer grew up in.

In other product categories there may be opportunities to sell subscriptions, which encourages habitual buying, or there may be opportunities to establish monthly payment deductions from a bank account, not only encouraging habitual behavior but also reducing the risk of alert triggers intervening in the buying process.

An improved offer may lead to a loss of market share

Moving a consumer from habitual to considered buying represents a risk for any brand that has a significant following of habitual purchasers. We might think that improving the offer is a sure-fire way to keep these habitual buyers, but this may not be the case.

Let me illustrate the problem by using a simple example: say that a breakfast cereal manufacturer offers a standard cereal product that is largely bought habitually and enjoys a significant market share. Let's assume that this manufacturer then launches a new range of cereal products with various flavors, delivered by adding fruit or spices to the cereal.

This is the likely sequence of events for at least some – and possibly many – of the habitual buyers: the brand offers a number of new flavors, and this innovation is promoted as something that is really worth trying. So the consumer who routinely bought this brand may now try a new flavor.

When this happens the consumer first breaks their

habitual buying routine and, second, experiences the benefit of variety. As a consequence, they may well recognize the benefit of not always buying the same product without thinking. To have something a little different may in fact turn out to be quite pleasant. The consequence is that the consumer may start to look for more change, more variety or even more excitement. And this means that the consumer starts to move from habitual purchasing to purchasing that is directed by a goal: in this case, to enjoy novelty.

At this point, the consumer is likely to consider other brands as well. After all, they were never really brand loyal – they were just making a habitual purchase, and so there is no barrier to change. The established habit has been replaced with a dedicated search for new flavor experiences, and the search is not limited to the brand that was previously bought habitually.

This sequence of events explains why brands that rely largely on habitual buying need to be very careful when pushing the consumer into a conscious purchase decision, especially when introducing the consumer to the joys of variety. Having said that, it is equally important for brands to be ready with interesting options and new experiences for when the consumer decides to seek these out. Brands also need to innovate to stay fresh and ensure they don't mature.

The challenge is this: marketers relying largely on habitual purchases don't want to encourage their own habitually buying consumers to change, but they do want to encourage consumers who habitually purchase competitive brands to change. At the same time, they want to make sure that consumers who are already looking for change are attracted to their brand.

Other significant implications include:
- You need to focus on behavior rather than attitudes or beliefs. Habits occur through the repetition of behavior and remain stable over time. Attitudes and beliefs are transitory and difficult to translate into predictable action.

- Training the habitual mind is different to 'educating' the conscious mind. The conscious mind can learn through reason and intention, while the habitual mind learns through repetition and reward.
- Habits are activated by triggers. Marketing communications and shopper marketing initiatives can be designed to trigger habitual buying.
- When consumers buy your brand on a habitual basis, you don't want them to think about this purchase. If the consumer starts thinking consciously about the purchase, they may well also start to consider alternative brands and products.
- If you want to preserve habitual buying, you need to make sure that every aspect of the offer and how it is delivered is within the buyer's expectations. Any significant change in any aspect of your offer – such as its pricing, distribution or promotion – can activate the conscious mind, and once the thinking mind is involved the purchase is no longer habitual.
- On the positive side, if you want habitual purchasing to continue, consider that strongly entrenched habits are hard to change. When companies reduce the quality of a product or service, we typically don't see a mass defection. A large majority of customers continue to buy the product pretty much the same way they always have. Losses are usually less than 5% above normal attrition.
- However, to gain market share in a category where purchasing is largely habitual, you will have to get your competitors' customers to think about their purchase. Strongly entrenched habits are difficult to break. You will need to make a significant effort to first get the consumer's conscious mind to make the change and to then habitualize the new behaviour; in this case, the purchase of your brand.

Breaking habits

Habits can be broken more easily when a change carries *low risk*, requires *low effort* and results in *immediate rewards*:

- **Low risk**: The consumer does not have to make a

significant investment that could result in losses if the new option turns out to be less rewarding than expected. Clearly, this is the case with many FMCG purchases. If the new brand or product doesn't deliver as expected, the consumer simply switches back to the one they used to buy habitually before, and their loss is minimal.
- **Low effort**: In some countries, changing a financial institution is a messy and complicated undertaking, requiring many forms to be completed and details to be secured. This leads to consumers staying with a financial institution even if they are no longer happy with their choice.
- **Immediate rewards**: When switching to another brand or product, the new choice is more likely to become habitualized if the consumer gets immediate positive rewards such as enjoyable flavors or useful new features, leading to repeat purchases.

This would all be pretty straightforward – if we didn't have to contend with competitors! As I have already stated, the marketing challenge consists of:
- Get the habitual buyers of competing brands to consciously consider their purchase (which is essential to getting them to switch to your brand).
- At *the same time* discourage habitual buyers of your brand from consciously considering their purchase, because making the purchase conscious may lead them to try a competing brand.

As I have already mentioned, the problem with product variations, new product features, discounts, and other initiatives based on an aspect of the traditional marketing mix is that all of these strategies may bring the purchase into the consumer's conscious thinking. And when the habitual buyers of your own brand start to consider their purchase consciously, the risk is that they will also consider competitive brands.

I will present a disruption strategy in Chapter 8. At this stage I will limit myself to a couple of more generic options.

Avoid a conscious decision by engaging only the nonconscious mind

A long time ago I used to believe that we needed to get the consumer's attention to be effective. My thinking – which was very much aligned with that of most other marketers - followed the AIDA formula: Attention, Interest, Desire, Action. Today, I know that exposures, including advertising, can work effectively even when the consumer is not aware of them. This includes exposures related to low involvement products to which the consumer often pays little or no attention.

There are a multitude of experiments that demonstrate this fact. Here are some examples:

- In one experiment, participants were asked to read some text displayed in the middle of a computer screen and to follow their reading with their mouse cursor. In addition to the text in the center of the screen, there were ads displayed on the left border. When asked, after they completed their reading tasks, participants could not recall any of the ads. Afterwards, however, they chose the advertised brands significantly more often than did a control group.
- In a test, participants were asked to review ads shown on a screen that also displayed, at the bottom, a stock ticker with share prices, gains and losses for various corporations. When asked after the test, participants could not recall any of the stock information. However, in a subsequent share portfolio game, those exposed to the stock information of particular firms more often bought the shares that had been displayed with positive information in the ticker and thus did much better than the control group.
- You are most likely not aware that your eyes are constantly scanning the periphery. In fact, they are moving on average twice per second without your even registering it. This again shows that our non-conscious mind is constantly gathering information, much of which will be discarded of course, but some

of which will be stored in memory.

The key point is that, in these situations, your mind processes signals without you being aware of it. Many purchases are habitual, and most signals sent by marketing communications, logos, packaging, POS material, promotions, etc., are processed by the nonconscious. This means that logic does not enter the equation, because the nonconscious mind cannot apply logic. Rather, the signals are processed with the help of learned codes (as discussed earlier) and other memory patterns that help the nonconscious mind decide whether or not a signal is worth retaining in memory.

The fact that the consumer's brain processes the vast majority of signals nonconsciously means that you can use very subtle messages and trust that they will in fact be received by the nonconscious mind.

For many marketers, this is anathema. Marketing efforts generally aim at getting the consumer's attention, yet here I am recommending exposing consumers to messages that stay at the nonconscious level. The reason for this recommendation, however, is obvious: as long as the consumer processes these messages with the nonconscious mind, you can avoid upsetting their habitual purchase behavior.

This means that you can change how the consumer thinks and feels about your brand, and shape their purchase decisions, without them being aware of it. Strategies and tactics of this nature are typically grouped together under the heading 'Behavioral Economics'. If you feel that's farfetched, then go back to the previous examples illustrating how exposures the consumer is not aware of can nevertheless have a significant impact on their behavior. You can also find a range of examples in the chapter on Shopper Marketing.

Habits may precede attitudes

Before I leave the topic of habitual buying I need to cover one more aspect: I suggested earlier that a habitual buyer would have made a purchase decision before habitualizing their behavior, possibly many years ago. However, this is actually not always the case: they may have bought what they got used to while living with their parents; they may have chosen something that was on special; they may have made a random selection and never bothered to compare the product or service they buy with other options open to them. In other words, *they never made a purchase decision at all.* Rather, they used a shortcut that eliminated the need to make a decision.

Consider a typical example: you have just started an office-based job that takes you into the CBD and, when lunchtime comes, you need to find a place to have a light lunch. You look up and down the street your office is on and see a Starbucks. You feel a sense of familiarity and, while you are not a loyal Starbucks customer, you decide it's as good a place as any and have your lunch there.

The place turns out to be quite comfortable, the coffee and sandwich okay – so you go back the next day, and the day after that. Over time, you develop a habit: when you have lunch alone you tend to go to the Starbucks down the street without even thinking.

A year or so later you participate in a survey and are asked where you most often have your lunch and the reasons for your choice. You are not likely to say *'Well, I just went there by accident and then kept going back because it was OK. I don't really know if there are better options around here as I never tried other places. So I guess all I can say is that this place is fit for purpose – it may not be the best one, I might like another place better, but I've never bothered to try!'*

If you are like most consumers you will look for positive features or aspects you like and present these as the reason for preferring this lunch place. However, these are not the reasons for you selecting this place to start with. You have simply selected a place that was convenient. You have not undertaken a proper review of different options you could have chosen instead, so you don't know if the place you frequent is the best place for you, but over time you have developed positive attitudes. In other words, *your behavior preceded your positive attitudes*. You feel good about this place *because* you have been going there for a long time, rather than having started to go there because you felt good about the place.

This happens quite frequently. Consumers pick a brand – typically without knowing why – get used to it, start buying habitually, and when asked why they consistently buy that brand they will come up with all sorts of rationalizations. From a neuromarketing perspective we can say that their choice was driven by their non-conscious mind, but they now use their conscious mind to rationalize what they are doing.

Part II
Strategic considerations

This book is about applying neuroscience-based concepts, tools and methodologies to the development and execution of brand strategies. However, not every step in brand strategy development and execution can benefit in the same way from a neuro perspective.

A challenge all marketers face when making strategic decisions is how to avoid your own bias. Intuition can be an invaluable tool for successful marketers, but you don't want your nonconscious mind simply taking shortcuts that do not deliver the best possible outcome. At the same time you don't want to rely solely on a 'rational' assessment as your conscious, rational mind is quite limited in scope and cannot deal with multiple concepts concurrently. What a dilemma!

There are ways you can boost your chances of making solid decisions:

First, do not look at analysis as benefitting only your conscious mind. Sure enough, it is a conscious activity, but the memory patterns your nonconscious mind develops as you carry out your analyses will also inform your nonconscious in the future. In fact, the more you analyze and explore, the more memories you create, allowing your nonconscious to explore a much richer landscape. Having more experience, exploring and analyzing more extensively will therefore benefit your intuition and boost your creativity.

Second, when your intuition is suggesting you pursue certain directions, solutions or opportunities ask yourself if this is likely to be based on experiences and knowledge that have resulted in useful memory patterns, or if it is more likely to be a shortcut your nonconscious is serving up because it is unable to understand the challenge you are facing. There is no sure-fire way for you to know where your gut feeling comes from, but a useful test is to ask yourself how much relevant experience you have.

Years ago, when the internet was still quite new, we saw a lot of investment into start-up companies that ended up as flops. The problem was that there was no experience base. Traditionally companies were valued on the basis of financial performance. These new internet firms, however, suggested that attracting large numbers of visitors or users would lead to a massive future cashflow. Blinded by these numbers, and with no experience base to draw on, many investors lost their money. Today, we see the same scenario playing out with cryptocurrencies. There is no experience base and it would be surprising if this bubble plays out differently to the dot.com bubble a couple of decades ago.

What I am suggesting is that you should consider if your gut feelings or intuition are likely to be based on actual experience and knowledge, i.e., on potentially useful memories, or not. If not, you should double up on gathering data and analyzing options rather than give much weight to what your intuition is telling you. In the former case, however, you should listen carefully to your gut feelings and seriously explore the directions or solutions that feel right.

Third, avoid group think. It is important to get different inputs and views but you need to be careful that you structure the process to avoid too-early adoption of a specific direction. Here are some of the things you should (and shouldn't) do:

When you have a working session, always ask participants to do some homework beforehand. They should go through their own analyzes and bring their views to the meeting, ideally in a format that can be posted on the meeting room walls. This will avoid everybody simply following the direction set by the most senior executive, the first person to speak, or the most forceful participant.

Go through different views first, before entering into any evaluation. This allows everyone to tell their story rather than being constantly interrupted and side-tracked by comments others may have to offer.

When evaluating ideas, direction, concepts or suggestions ask first for positive comments only. Everybody should try to find something that is positive about what has been put forward, even if they don't agree with the overall proposition. This is an important first step – it frees up thinking (by exploring positives and negatives) and also creates a positive work environment that encourages out-of-the-box suggestions.

Focus not only on differences between options, but also on similarities. This may allow you to find solutions that cover more territory or are simply stronger because they consider a wider range of factors.

One of the most important points is that you should ban the use of PowerPoint slides unless someone needs to show an illustration, such as a flowchart or table. PowerPoint slides are for people who lack imagination or can't string a story together. They fragment the message and encourage a serial approach to thinking, rather than allowing the audience to get immersed in the story and to grasp the complexity of what is being put forward. Furthermore, there is far too much effort invested into making PowerPoint presentations look pretty, putting form above substance. Surely you want a working session with substance rather than just pretty slides.

While PowerPoints are arguably the worst way to communicate it is also important to avoid recording key points on a whiteboard, as this will set the direction for the meeting. Of course, it is useful to record the outcomes and the underlying reasons *once some conclusions have been reached*, but that's different to putting key points on a board while the group is still exploring, thereby focusing the group's attention on what is on the board rather than encouraging them to explore widely.

Needless to say, you should provide all team members with any required readings or information well before the working session. This allows them to explore the challenge in their conscious mind by thinking about it, and in their nonconscious mind that will make connections between memories that may lead to new insights, concepts and directions.

The saying 'sleep on it' may sound like a throw-away line but it is actually very valuable advice. While you sleep your brain will review memories, build new connections and create new patterns that can lead to new insights and creative solutions. If you provide information just before – or, worse – during the work session, you are conditioning the conscious mind to focus narrowly on whatever it is you have provided, without the benefit of any nonconcious exploration.

With this brief introduction to avoiding bias and narrow thinking when developing brand strategies, I will now move on to concepts and tools that can contribute to developing an effective brand strategy. There are two core challenges:

First, to develop high-level strategies that ensure the return from your brand *portfolio* is optimized. This requires you to *consider all brands concurrently*. I will take you through a **SWOT Exploration** that delivers the broadest perspective, taking into account internal and external factors while aiming at developing a high-level strategic direction. This is followed by an overview on **brand portfolio planning**, identifying strategic directions based on the life cycle of your brands. The final section rounds off the portfolio approach with a methodology you can use to **minimize cannibalization** within your brand portfolio while **maximizing competitive differentiation**.

As I mentioned earlier, all these analyzes take a *portfolio* view. Once the role of each brand within your portfolio has been nailed down it is time to consider each brand individually.

I will take you through a number of **disruption** concepts to help you explore whether any of your brands could benefit from disruption. This is followed by a chapter on **brand vision archetypes** as an important means of creating a consistent brand image in the market place and, finally, **strategic segmentation**.

6 SWOT Exploration: identifying high-level strategic options

Exploring Strengths, Weaknesses, Opportunities and Threats can be extremely useful when facing a complex strategic challenge as long as you do not limit yourself to just an analytical assessment, but rather systematically explore strategic options.

The SWOT Exploration should be about lateral thinking - identifying key issues and then exploring relationships between external and internal factors that may not have been obvious, thus leading to new insights and strategic directions. Such an exploration can be carried out at various levels of aggregation - for a single product or brand, a product or brand portfolio, the marketing department/agency, the marketing program, or the whole company/agency.

How does it work?
The SWOT analysis is one of the most widely used - but also one of the most abused - concepts. Let me therefore start with a list of common pitfalls when carrying out a SWOT.

1. *Strategic focus*
When you identify the four key aspects – Strengths, Weaknesses, Opportunities and Threats – you need to take a strategic perspective. This is not an exercise in completeness, but in creating a foundation for making strategic decisions. It follows that you need to focus on what is *important*, rather than try to develop a long list of Strengths, Weaknesses, Opportunities and Threats that will only serve to bury the few important aspects under a rubble of meaningless points. In most cases there are only five or six items that are worth listing under each heading.

2. *Opportunities and Threats*
You should start with *Opportunities and Threats* and list only the most important ones.

At this stage a common mistake is to list things you *might do*, i.e., actions and strategic options. However, *an Opportunity is not something you could do, but rather a development that is not under your control.* In other words, it is something that happens in your operating environment. Forget what you might do about the external developments you identify. Rather, simply identify them and then decide if they are most likely Opportunities or Threats and list them accordingly.

This is important, so I will say it again: *do not include any actions or strategies in your list of Opportunities.* If you do that, you will ignore many different ways of dealing with a particular Opportunity or Threat by focusing from the beginning on only one particular strategic option. To illustrate this point:

Let's assume you are marketing a range of breakfast foods. Naturally, you are aware of the obesity crisis and the fact that a growing percentage of the population is becoming overweight or obese.

If you decided to put 'promote how our low calorie breakfast food helps consumers to manage their weight' under Opportunities you have firstly failed to identify the real opportunity (or threat) – namely the obesity crisis – and, most importantly, you have already decided without any further exploration that your strategy will be to emphasize that your product is a low calorie one.

There are, of course, many other strategic options you could have explored, such as:
- *promoting your breakfast food as keeping you going for longer because of its low glycemic index (low GI)*
- *positioning your breakfast food as indulgent, i.e., going with the trend rather than against it – after all, more people out there are eating more, that's why we have an obesity crisis*
- *offering your food in single serving sizes to help with portion control*
- *emphasizing the need to have a good breakfast because skipping breakfast is associated with weight gain.*

Your decision on which strategy to pursue should not be made at this early stage. Right now, you should record the broader Opportunities and Threats rather than what you might do about them. It follows that you should try to identify relevant changes you expect to occur with respect to industry sectors, competitors, distribution channels, consumer segments, media, technology, and so on. It doesn't matter that you won't know exactly how these changes will play out. At this early stage, you are simply highlighting that you expect some significant changes to occur.

It is also entirely possible that a particular development represents both an Opportunity and a Threat. If that's the case, list it under both headings.

3. *Strengths and Weaknesses*
Once you have identified Opportunities and Threats, move on to considering your Strengths and Weaknesses, i.e., where your company, brands, skill sets, resources, processes, relationships, assets, etc. either deliver advantages or are holding you back.

It is important to keep in mind that being particularly good at something does not necessarily mean it is a Strength. If, say, all your competitors are just as good at it as you are, then clearly you don't have a competitive strength. Similarly, *being quite bad at something does not necessarily have to be a Weakness.* Again, if nobody can do better than you, then this lack of excellence does not constitute a competitive weakness. To illustrate this point:

Let's assume you are highly price competitive due to a modern manufacturing plant, but you lack distribution in one of the main retail channels.

If your competitors are also highly price competitive because they too have modern manufacturing facilities, or access to cheaper raw materials, or can spread overheads across larger volumes, then 'being highly price competitive' is not a Strength. If your competitors also have only limited market coverage then your limited distribution is not a Weakness.

In other words, Strengths and Weaknesses are relative

rather than absolute in nature. And, most importantly, what is a Strength and what is a Weakness can only be established in the context of the Opportunities and Threats you are facing. For example, a premium price positioning may have been a Strength during boom financial times, but may have to be placed under Weaknesses when a recessionary period takes hold.

The SWOT Grid
You should use a grid to record your assessment:

Note: adopt a strategic view and focus on the most important issues only!!!	Opportunities (list)	Threats (list)
Strengths (list)		
Weaknesses (list)		

Illustration 5: The SWOT Grid

Identifying strategic directions
One of the most common misuses of the SWOT concept is to stop with the list of Strengths, Weaknesses, Opportunities and Threats. Once you have completed the task of identifying and listing SWOTs as you see them, you need to explore what you might do about them. This is the first time during this exercise that you should think about strategic directions and actions. Up to this point, you should have simply identified important external developments (Opportunities and Threats) and

internal attributes (Strengths and Weaknesses).

You need to think laterally, but identifying what you might do should not be done in a brainstorming session. What you need at this stage is sound strategic thinking rather than just a bunch of ideas. Be systematic and explore what actions you could take, given the unique mix of external and internal factors you have identified. It is important that you don't develop full-fledged strategies at this point, but rather record some core strategic directions that can be explored more fully at a later stage.

The four sections in the right, lower part of the grid (see Figure 2) allow you to consider the relationships between Opportunities and Strengths, Threats and Strengths, Opportunities and Weaknesses, and Threats and Weaknesses. This is the fundamental exercise of a SWOT Exploration. Clearly, you and your team need to spend time exploring how you might exploit Opportunities, which Strengths you may be able to leverage and which Weaknesses you may have to correct to be able to exploit these Opportunities.

Note: *adopt a strategic view and focus on the most important issues only!!!*	Opportunities (list)	Threats (list)
Strengths (list)	Can we build on our strengths to exploit any of these opportunities? Is there something we should/could do? Write strategies and actions into this square....	Are some of these threats weakening specific strengths we have today? If yes, is there something we should/could do? Write strategies and actions into this square....
Weaknesses (list)	Are there some great opportunities we can't exploit because of particular weaknesses? If so, what could/should we do? Write strategies and actions into this square....	Could some of these threats hit us where we are already weak? If so, what should/could we do? Write strategies and actions into this square....

Illustration 6: *Relationships between SWOTs*

Most importantly, a SWOT should not be about 'completeness'. I have already mentioned that you should only consider Strengths, Weaknesses, Opportunities and Threats that are of strategic importance, rather than try to develop a long list of all the factors you can think of. The same applies to exploring possible strategic directions and options: you do not need a strategy for every combination of your Strengths and Weaknesses against Opportunities and Threats. Rather, your task is to *identify the combinations that open up a major strategic opportunity*.

There will be some Strengths that don't line up with Opportunities – that's fine, just ignore them. Similarly, ignore Opportunities you can't exploit because you don't have any particular Strengths to do so and can't realistically develop them. The same applies to Threats and Weaknesses. The challenge is not to become the 'perfect' organization or brand by eliminating all Weaknesses, but rather to deal with those that represent grave strategic risks or truly stand in the way of exploiting key opportunities.

Sometimes a *core strategy* surfaces that allows you to address a number of challenges simultaneously. This does not happen often but, when it does, it typically requires a fundamental move such as focusing on a consumer segment or distribution channel you have not given much (or any) attention in the past. Core strategies can be a highly effective and efficient way of exploiting the changing environment. It is worthwhile spending a bit of time trying to identify such a strategy.

Using your SWOT to evaluate initiatives and strategies

It is not uncommon to find brands, products, communications, marketing or business strategies that seem to build on weaknesses rather than threats and/or fail to exploit opportunities. Most often, this is the outcome of an incremental decision-making process that tends to focus on detail rather than the big strategic context. The SWOT Exploration can help you ensure strategy is at the core of all decisions.

Simply consider any significant investment into your brands, products, communications or marketing in light of your SWOT. Ask yourself these obvious questions:
- Are we really building on our Strengths or rectifying a Weakness that is a strategic barrier to progress?
- Are we actually exploiting a key Opportunity with the planned move or are we just fiddling around the edges?
- Will this initiative make us more vulnerable down the track?
- Are there any Threats that could turn this initiative into a disaster?

A well-developed SWOT Exploration will very quickly highlight if you are chasing after insignificant incremental improvements or capitalizing effectively on the opportunities open to you.

Keeping your SWOT up-to-date
This leads me to another key point: as you are operating in a fluid environment with constant changes on the market and competitive fronts, you need to review and update your SWOT regularly.

The good news is that keeping your SWOT up-to-date does not require much time or energy. It is simply a matter of adjusting your SWOT every time there is a significant change in the external operating environment or your company that would affect your brand(s). Needless to say, significant changes in the operating environment may also have an impact on your strengths and weaknesses. It is therefore good practice to review the latter whenever you re-assess your key opportunities and threats.

A highly effective means of updating your SWOT is to place the grid (in supersize) in a meeting room or office, together with a stack of Post-It! Notes, allowing any of your colleagues who identify new developments or insights that may deserve attention to add these to the grid without delay. Once this dynamic works, you will find that the grid becomes a frequent center for discussions and explorations. These can be held informally, possibly with a formal update session whenever you feel that's warranted.

7 Defining the strategic direction across your brand portfolio

If you want to optimize your marketing investment you have to develop a portfolio strategy that delivers the best outcomes across all of the brands in your portfolio. Optimizing each brand strategy in isolation is not likely to get you there – in fact, it will likely to lead to a sub-optimal outcome as you overinvest in brands that give you a smaller early return, extract too much revenue from mature brands you should keep alive and milk longer-term, and overinvest in opportunities rather than being selective in your choices. A concept that can help you develop a well-integrated strategy is Portfolio Analysis.

The McKinsey portfolio concept
The following illustration shows a portfolio grid. You can see that there are four quadrants – *Question Mark*, *Star*, *Cash Cow* and *Dog*. Depending on which quadrant your brand falls into, there are specific standard strategies that typically work for brands in these respective portfolio positions.

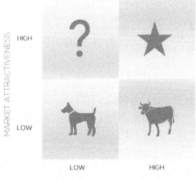

Illustration 7: *Portfolio Grid*

You will have noted the two dimensions of the portfolio grid: *market attractiveness* and *relative competitive advantage*. Brands (or products) are positioned on this grid according to the attractiveness of the markets they are competing in, and the extent to which they enjoy a relative advantage compared to their major competitors. You therefore need to make a number of decisions when conducting a Portfolio Analysis, including:

Market attractiveness
Here you need to take a corporate rather than a brand-specific view, as your company should seek to build a portfolio of brands that allows it to compete in the most attractive markets.

Relative competitive advantage
Typically the key factors that provide a brand with a relative competitive advantage are the same across most categories, including aspects such as a large market share; market share growth; market coverage; and repeat (or even habitual) purchases. However, if the competitive advantage factors are vastly different between brands competing in different markets then the use of brand-specific factors is warranted.

Once you have identified what your market attractiveness and relative competitive advantage factors are, you can assess each of your brands against these criteria using a rating scale, and their total score across all these criteria will determine where they should be placed on the portfolio grid. If you feel that some criteria are more important than others you can weight your set of criteria. It is however important to only include criteria you believe have a material impact on your brand's success. In most cases four to five criteria for each of the two dimensions of the grid are sufficient.

With your brands located in the various quadrants of the grid you need to ask yourself what the most promising *strategic direction* is for each one of your brands. Your ability to advance the brands in your portfolio will be restrained by resource limitations. Investing more into one brand will limit the resources available to another.

This is exactly what makes portfolio analysis so useful: it forces you to develop strategies and allocate resources *concurrently* for all brands, taking their particular positions on the grid – and thus their strategic role and potential – into account.

Interpreting the portfolio
There are standard strategies that tend to work better for brands that find themselves in different positions on the grid. It is, however, important to recognize that these are just *standard strategies* – think of them as being the right strategies in perhaps 80% of cases. Your challenge is to work out if your brand is one of these, or one of the 20% of exceptions.

This requires exploration – you should never follow the standard strategies without thinking, as this can lead to disaster. When you feel you should deviate from a standard strategy *you need to present a compelling argument as to why your brand is an exception and thus should not follow what works in 80% of cases.*

The standard strategies for each of the four quadrants follow the concept of the brand or product life cycle:

When you launch a new brand you are likely to choose an attractive market to launch it into, but your relative competitive advantage is not likely to be strong to start with. This means your brand ends up in the *Question Mark* position. When a company has several brands in this position it makes sense to select the most promising one(s) to invest in while putting other opportunities on ice or even closing them down. This ensures that the most promising brands are not starved of resources because you are spreading your limited resources too thinly across too many brands.

When a Question Mark brand strengthens its competitive position it develops into a *Star*. Stars deserve investment but because they are typically growing they will eat up most – perhaps even all – of the cash-flow they generate. In other words, they are unlikely to be major providers of free cash-flow.

However, as a Star brand matures it will move into the *Cash Cow* position – typically as a major mature brand that is past its growth phase but is now generating significant free cash-flow. You should invest into your Cash Cow only as much as is necessary to protect it, and only as long as it still generates free cash-flow that can be invested into promising Question Mark brands, or into supporting the growth of Stars.

Finally, as a Cash Cow's competitive advantage diminishes it ends up as a *Dog* and you should consider divesting it. Sometimes it is best to simply take the brand off the market, sometimes there is an opportunity to keep the price up – or even lift it - and accept decreasing volumes while still generating a positive cash-flow. What you should *not* do is to enter into price competition as your ultimate goal is to divest Dog brands because they lack potential.

In summary the standard strategies are:

Question mark Selectively invest/divest

Star Invest

Cash Cow Protect (invest as much as required to keep the Cash Cow going but don't overinvest because it has no long-term future) and milk

Dog Divest – either rapidly, or let the Dog die slowly while still generating positive margins, but avoid competing on price at all costs as you are not trying to maintain your market share.

Conducting a portfolio analysis and reviewing the portfolio directions can help you lift the return on marketing investment by optimizing your brand portfolio, rather than dealing with each brand in isolation despite the fact that they are all resourced by the same – limited – budget.

Brand positioning strategies

Portfolio analysis is a great tool when it comes to developing a fully aligned set of strategies for all your brands. There is, however, an important issue that portfolio analysis does not address explicitly: identifying possible cannibalizations within your brand portfolio and maximizing the competitive differentiation of any competing brands.

The first step is to be clear about the role different brand attributes, qualities and capabilities play (I will use 'attributes' in future as shorthand for all these elements). Specifically, which attributes represent entry requirements, i.e., permission to play, and which help to build a competitive advantage.

Often the entry requirements are known. Many will relate to the product or service you offer – it has to be 'fit for purpose' or you won't be able to enter the market successfully. Some are related to your brand. For example 'trust' is typically an entry requirement. Consumers are unlikely to consider your brand if they don't trust it.

All too often entry requirements are treated as though they were offering a competitive advantage. Just because consumers won't buy a brand they don't trust does not mean that trust allows you to build a competitive advantage. Once you have a trusted brand you have to compete on the basis of other attributes.

There are, of course, always exceptions. For example, in China trust is a major differentiating factor for baby formula due to contamination scandals that made thousands of babies sick and led to the death of some. In that market, consumers are influenced by how much they trust a brand when making a final purchase decision, elevating trust to a competitive differentiation factor.

To develop your portfolio strategy you need to know:
- What are the key entry requirements, i.e., the must-have attributes the consumer expects any acceptable brand to deliver?
- Which attributes are key competitive differentiation factors?

- To what degree are different brands (your own and your competitors' brands) seen to 'own' these key competitive differentiation attributes?

The portfolio grid is an excellent tool, but it is not designed to clarify which territory different brands 'own' in the consumer's mind. Yet this is an essential consideration when it comes to developing a brand strategy.

For example, you may want to minimize cannibalization within your portfolio, have your brand take exclusive ownership of some territory in the consumer's mind, or share territory with a leading brand to weaken its dominance. Naturally, you want to make sure that you focus on territory that represents purchase drivers. There is no point in aiming to occupy territory that is 'nice to have' but does not result in additional market share.

There is a research tool that is easy to apply and affordable: The Response Time Test (RTT) allows you to identify the purchase drivers for a category and to ascertain which of these attributes are 'owned' by specific brands, which are shared by two or more brands, and which are still available. The RTT delivers insights that provide a solid foundation for a strategy that minimizes unwanted cannibalization amongst the brands in your portfolio while maximizing desirable competitive differentiation from your competitors' brands.

The Response Time Test

Consumers connect some brands with particular qualities that are essential to satisfying their goals. For example, Apple is often connected with 'innovation' and a consumer who wants to feel or project that they are innovative, smart and/or different is likely to be drawn to the Apple brand.

The RTT assesses *how strongly* specific qualities, attributes or capabilities are connected to brands in the consumer's mind, by measuring the time it takes the consumer to agree that a brand and an attribute are related (i.e., they 'make sense'). The underlying neuroscience foundation is the fact that memory patterns with strong neural connections trigger a fast response, while associations that are only tenuously connected make the consumer hesitate, resulting in a longer response time.

For example, consider showing a consumer a picture of an IBM (or a Lenovo, HP, Asus or other PC) logo together with the word 'innovative' and asking them to tap a particular key on a mobile, tablet or computer if the two elements go well together. Then repeat the exercise, but this time show the Apple logo and the word 'innovative'. You would expect that there is some hesitation in the first case. Of course you can do lots of creative things with a PC, but it is still likely that your respondent will hesitate just for a moment before pushing the button. With the Apple brand, however, there is – for many people – a much stronger neural connection between the memory patterns 'Apple' and 'innovative' which leads to a much faster response time. It follows that the reaction time measures how closely two concepts are connected in the consumer's mind.

You can also use the RTT to assess the impact of an advertising campaign that aims to associate a particular quality with your brand. A successful campaign should reduce the reaction time measured by the RTT when it comes to testing the association of your brand and this quality. Comparing the results of an RTT conducted before and after the campaign, respectively, will provide you with a measure of success.

The RTT can be administered online, via computer or by smart phone. An initial calibration ensures that download and reading speed and the average speed a consumer responds with are factored into the measurement of response times assessed by the survey.

The following case example illustrates how the RTT can identify the key purchase drivers in your category and the strength of the associations between your and your competitors' brands and these purchase drivers. The example will illustrate the methodology using a couple of brands only. You will most likely need to cover a larger number of brands, but the approach will stay the same.

Illustration
What is driving purchase decisions? Which attributes should you focus on? [5]

With household cleaning products effectiveness is a key issue, but this may be an entry requirement rather than a competitive differentiator. That is, consumers would not buy a cleaning product they believe is not effective, but there are a number of brands that are seen to deliver on this front. Being effective merely means a brand is an acceptable choice rather than be differentiated from competitive brands that have also passed the entry test.

A leading brand was searching for any other vital factors besides effectiveness that might drive consumer purchase behavior. A comparative study including a major competitive brand was undertaken, testing nine attributes as follows:

Ingredients
- guarantee of quality
- is eco-friendly
- contains bleach

Effectiveness
- cleans effectively
- cleans fast
- kills all germs

Comfort
- is ready to use
- has comfortable packaging
- is easy to store

The study assessed the profile of an ideal household cleaner and then proceeded to assess the strength of

---

[5] Adapted from Michal Matukin and Rafal Ohme, *How Reaction Time Measurement Empowers Marketing and Market Research*, in Paul Dovas et. al., *Market Research Revolution. A Marketer's Guide to Emerging New Methods*, NMSBA 2017, p. 9

associations between the identified purchase drivers and specific brands. The following chart shows the aggregate results for an ideal cleaning product. You can see two types of responses captured in the chart: the *explicit measure* shows the percentage of respondents who gave a particular answer; the *implicit measure*, shown as a color-code, indicates how quickly respondents gave their answer. The implicit responses have been categorized into 'not sure at all' (black), 'somewhat unsure' (dark grey), and 'absolutely certain' (light grey).

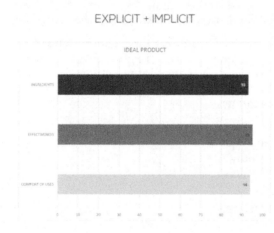

Illustration 8: *RTT results for household cleaner category*

Despite the high *explicit* score – all above 90% - *implicit* results indicate that consumers do not truly care about *'ingredients'* and the high explicit score is just lip service (the black color indicates lack of certainty). '*Effectiveness'* scores high on conscious evaluation for the ideal product, but the Reaction Time indicates only moderate certainty (dark grey). What really matters is '*comfort of usage'* as consumers were sure when answering, i.e., they did not hesitate.

The scores achieved by two respective brands were:

Illustration 9: *RTT results for household cleaner brands*

Both brands A and B were rated highly with respect to '*effectiveness*'. What sets brand A apart, however, is '*comfort of usage*', where consumers believe – with a high degree of certainty – that brand A performs well, while they are only moderately certain that brand B delivers. Fortunately for Brand A '*comfort of usage*' is one of the most important drivers for the entire household cleaner category.

Clearly brand A should focus on '*comfort of usage*', attempting to take ownership of this important attribute while continuing to remind consumers that it also delivers on '*effectiveness*'. This will ensure that the brand maintains parity with B on this attribute while making it impossible for B to take ownership of '*effectiveness*'.

What this illustration – based on real-world data – shows is that the RTT allows you to evaluate the conviction with which respondents answer your questions. In this case the RTT identified the key purchase drivers and the strength of the associations different brands enjoy with these purchase drivers. Strong neuronal connections speed up response times, allowing us to use the RTT to assess to what degree consumers truly associate a brand with certain qualities and capabilities. Obviously, consumers are not aware of the relative strengths of neural connections so they could not tell us explicitly in a standard survey questionnaire how strongly they believe in their answers.

8 Disruption strategies

There are four disruption strategies every marketer should be aware of.

You have established the opportunities you plan to pursue and the threats you need to address with your SWOT Exploration. You have decided on the role each one of your brands needs to play in doing so with your Portfolio Analysis. And you have gained insights into the way your (and your competitors') brands are currently positioned in the consumer's mind, allowing you to develop brand strategies that minimize the cannibalization of your own brands while optimizing competitive differentiation, via a Response Time Test.

Informed by these analyzes you now have to make another strategic decision: should you disrupt current market and competitive conventions or should you fit in with the way the market has evolved, which typically means making only incremental improvements to your strategy? The answer will depend to quite some degree on the position your brand enjoys in the market place.

Dominant brands tend to have larger marketing budgets, better distribution, enjoy a higher degree of familiarity or even brand preference, are often able to tie up the most desirable partners when it comes to collaboration and sponsorships, find it easier to get media exposure and attract the best marketers and agencies. As dominant brands have tremendous natural advantages, they are typically well advised to maintain the status quo. They would not benefit from changing market or competitive conventions as this may diminish their dominance. It follows that if you have a challenger brand and you copy the strategies of the market leaders you are in fact playing into their hands: the last thing they want you to do is to disrupt the way things are!

The exception, of course, is when dominant brands lose ground, become obsolete and commoditize. This may be due to consumers growing bored with the old established brands and looking for something new and different, or a competitor pursuing a disruptive strategy. Either way, when the brand's natural advantages deteriorate it is time to consider a new, more aggressive, and possibly even disruptive strategy.

If you are responsible for a challenger brand or a *maturing* dominant brand you need to find a strategy that allows you to make a big, disruptive impact, to leapfrog (at least some of) your competitors or to re-vitalize your maturing dominant brand. And let me assure you, the strategy you choose will have a determining impact on the level of success you will enjoy.

It follows that your choice of strategy needs to be given serious consideration. Incremental strategies are usually not very demanding from a strategic point of view (although the execution may of course require a large dose of creativity). For this reason I will focus on disruption, where a number of highly effective concepts can guide your efforts.

The key question you need to answer is 'Which strategy should I choose?' or 'What are the strategic options open to me?' Exploring the various strategy concepts presented in the following pages should enable you to identify the one that serves you best given your current competitive, market and broader operating environments and your ambitions for your brand.

Here is a brief overview on the key concepts I will cover:

Blue Ocean Strategy
The Blue Ocean concept, developed by Kim & Mauborgne, is not about identifying a single differentiating factor that may set your brand or offer apart, but rather creating a *new competitive profile across the category's critical success factors.*

Cultural Strategy
Holt's cultural strategy concept focuses on *aligning your brand or product strategy with an emerging ideology during a time of cultural disruption.* This is a somewhat unconventional approach given that marketers typically focus on

the individual rather than taking a cultural perspective, but is highly topical as the world today is at the beginning of a major cultural disruption.

Changing the meaning of products and brands
Verganti suggests that *changing the meaning* of products can lead to powerful innovation and a repositioning of your brand.

Taking the relationship to a higher emotional level
Neuroscience has shown that consumers buy brands and products to address their goals. These goals are typically emotional in nature and work in the nonconscious mind. Taking a neuromarketing approach you can *identify relevant higher-level goals and convince the consumer that your brand addresses these goals in an effective way.* This strategy can be turbo-charged by encouraging the development of a *brand tribe*, resulting in members of the tribe adding to or strengthening their emotional involvement.

8.1 Blue Ocean strategy

Blue Ocean strategies often go beyond the boundaries of brand or even marketing decisions by uncovering potential business concept innovations. However, there are two reasons for covering this strategy development concept here:

First, Blue Ocean strategies often result in major cost advantages which, given the future operating environment I outlined in the introduction to this book, is obviously a highly desirable outcome. Here are a few examples:

- Zara's Blue Ocean model cut the industry-standard 8+ month cycle for new collections to just 6 weeks, allowing it to align its offer with the market's response and thus selling some 80% of its products at full price compared to the competition's average of only 40%. This means that Zara can price its products profitably at approximately 25% below competitive brands.
- Enterprise developed into the largest rental car company in the US by focusing on renting replacement vehicles paid for by accident insurance, eliminating costly infrastructure (such as airport stations) and marketing expenses.
- Jet pioneered unattended petrol stations, requiring only half as much margin per liter of gas.
- Walmart pioneered cross-docking, leading to massive cost savings.

Obviously, not all Blue Ocean strategies lead to massive cost advantages, but many do and it is a methodology you should consider if you are aiming at developing a new business concept that will allow you to become price leader.

Secondly, I think it is worthwhile mentioning Blue Ocean Strategies because they recognize a very important step in any strategic planning process, namely the need to abandon elements of your current operation or strategy if you want to add new elements. Far too often marketers load feature upon feature with rapidly decreasing incremental impact, while adding enormously to complexity and costs.

Red Oceans are typically characterized by cut-throat competition and commoditization, while in Blue Oceans the rules of competition are only starting to emerge and the first into the Blue Ocean will benefit from a lack of (direct) competition. In my view, the Blue Ocean concept delivers three important benefits:
- First, by offering a simple and compelling concept (and even terminology) Kim and Mauborgne have put disruption on the agenda of many CEOs and corporate boards as well as CMOs.
- Second, the concept provides a means of *visualizing* disruptive strategies and, by doing so, allows you to capture the essence of your strategy in a compelling form.
- Third, and arguably most important, it draws attention to the fact that a brand (or company) needs to develop a *differentiated profile*, rather than only be different with respect to a single attribute or quality. It is this holistic, all-encompassing approach that sets this concept apart from mainstream thinking.

A Blue Ocean strategy takes your company or brand into a unique market position, which means you don't have any direct competitors. I have said 'market position' rather than 'market' because quite often the Blue Ocean represents a new niche in a well-established, Red Ocean market.

The key steps in developing a Blue Ocean strategy are:

The strategy canvas
The first step is to 'paint' the strategy canvas. The horizontal dimension of the canvas comprises of all the key factors that determine the position of competitors in the industry. The vertical dimension represents a measure of intensity or 'how much' of a particular factor a company offers.

This assessment can be quantitative or qualitative, and I

see this as an inherent strength of this concept. Some strategic planning concepts simply ignore factors that can't be measured with some accuracy, which is of course nonsense. Kim and Mauborgne's approach considers what is important rather than what can be quantified. The other point worth making is that these factors can be of an internal or external nature. The simple but effective rule is: *if a factor is important, include it.*

The more broadly based focus on *'whatever determines the position of competitors in the industry sector'* opens the mind to considering a greater diversity of factors than might be put on the agenda when developing more narrowly focused, traditional brand strategies.

Here is a simple example showing the strategy canvas for US circus companies/offers. The principle factors are:
- price of admission
- star performers
- animal shows
- aisle concessions
- multiple show arenas
- fun and humor
- thrills and danger
- unique venue.

At the time this grid was drawn up there were a number of small regional circuses that were quite similar with respect to the factors listed above while a dominant competitor, Ringling Brothers, had its own unique profile that set it apart.

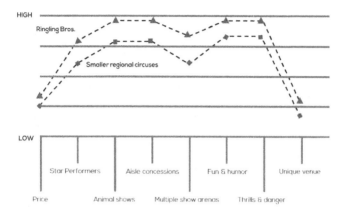

Illustration 10: *Strategy canvas – current situation*

We can use this strategy canvas to show how Cirque de Soleil found a Blue Ocean and came to dominate the circus industry by developing and offering a new concept that had never been seen before.

The six paths to creating Blue Oceans

There is, of course, a risk in not picking up factors that could serve as the basis for creating a new concept simply because we see them as fundamental to the category. For example, you could argue that Cirque de Soleil is not a circus at all because only shows that have animals fall into the circus category, or that aisle concessions are an essential feature of a circus because of the atmosphere they create.

From a commercial point of view this is clearly a redundant argument. The new concept may well redefine the category code, i.e., what people expect to experience when attending a circus performance. But there is a risk that factors that could have helped create a great new concept may have been ignored because of our rigid views about what falls into a category, in this case what is – and isn't – a circus.

Kim & Mauborgne's advice is to reconstruct market boundaries when you develop your Blue Ocean strategy. But thinking about market boundaries that could be changed is also a great way to complete your initial 'as is' strategy canvas. Here are the six market boundaries you should investigate (if they exist in your industry category):
1. alternative industries
2. strategic groups within industries (i.e., companies that pursue a similar strategy)
3. the chain of buyers – considering shifting focus to a party that has not been key in the past (e.g., a pharmaceuticals company focusing on patients rather than medical practitioners)
4. complementary product and service offerings
5. functional and emotional appeals to buyers
6. time, i.e., identify trends that will change value to customers.

The Four Actions framework
The second step is to consider which of the factors on your strategy canvas you should reduce, create, raise or eliminate. There is a tendency amongst executives to add, but not to subtract. This results in feature overload, which in turn results in an unfocused brand positioning and typically has a significant negative impact on the cost structure.

More specifically:
- Which of the factors that the industry takes for granted should be eliminated?
- Which factors should be reduced well below the industry standard?
- Which factors should be raised well above the industry standards?
- Which factors should be created that the industry has never offered?

The first two groups of factors allow you to reduce your cost. The final two questions are about lifting buyer value and creating new demand.

Here is the strategy canvas showing the impact of the Four Actions framework:

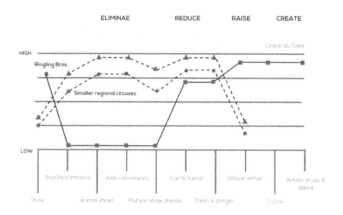

***Illustration 11:** Strategy canvas – Blue Ocean strategy*

Visualizing strategy

To an analytically minded person visualization may appear to be a superfluous effort, but anyone who has been in strategy presentations will have realized that it is much more compelling to 'see' a strategy than to just read about it. For a start you can bring all important elements together in one illustration (the strategy canvas) which allows the audience to grasp the all-important relationships between different elements of the strategy and to confirm in their mind that it is both fully integrated and internally consistent.

Kim and Mauborgne even suggest conducting a 'Strategy Fair' once you have developed alternative strategies, where you present the key decision-makers with visual representations of each option. Ideally, you establish stands or kiosks such as are used at conferences, where visual representations of the strategy are presented on large posters and team members answer questions.

Depending on the degree of confidentiality you may also want to invite some customers and even competitors' customers to review and provide feedback on the strategic solutions you have identified.

Characteristics of a good strategy

Kim and Mauborgne suggest that a good Blue Ocean Strategy has three features, namely:

- *Focus – a clear focus that is apparent from the strategy canvas*
  Limit the high values to a few aspects of the offering only. Otherwise you end up with a costly business model.
- *Divergence – a value curve that diverges from the industry sector's value curve*
  Differentiate your profile from the industry's average profile.
- *Compelling tagline – express what differentiates this company or brand in a compelling tagline*
  A good strategy can be compellingly summarized in just a few well-chosen words.

How to make best use of the Blue Ocean concept

The Blue Ocean concept facilitates high-level exploration. You can literally play with it and see where it takes you. By bringing all relevant aspects together on a single page you can explore core concepts for a corporate or product brand or simply different service mix options.

As always, however, there are also pitfalls. The most common problems I have come across include:

- A high degree of subjectivity when it comes to drawing the strategy canvas for your own brand, leading to a highly optimistic profile. This leads to a distorted strategy canvas which in turn may lead to ineffective strategies.
- A narrow focus on factors that are important to your brand rather than representative of the industry, market or product sector, potentially leading to a strategy that lacks wider impact.
- Taking an ideas-driven rather than exploratory

approach to the task, such as using brainstorming to simply generate an additional, new brand feature rather than developing a holistic, differentiated profile for your brand.
- Considering only your closest competitors rather than industry sector practices, as such a narrow focus may lead to missing some great opportunities.

For a detailed outline of the Blue Ocean concept read W. Chan Kim and Renée Mauborgne's earlier book *Blue Ocean Strategy, Expanded Edition: How to Create Uncontested Market Space and Make the Competition Irrelevant* (2015) and their latest: *Blue Ocean Shift: Beyond Competing – Proven Steps to Inspire Confidence and Seize New Growth* (2017).

8.2 Cultural Disruption

We see an obsession with global brands when it comes to case studies, conference presentations and publications. The focus is typically on what Nike, Apple, or some other global brand does. Sadly, these strategies aren't relevant to most marketers who do not manage global brands, but the prestige associated with these brands seems to be more important than the relevance of their strategies. What would be far more relevant and useful is to learn about how these once local, insignificant brands developed into global brands. Of course, market and competitive conditions are very different today compared to when these brands morphed into leading global brands, but the principles are still the same.

What makes Holt & Cameron's cultural disruption concept so exciting is that they focus on the early life of today's leading brands, exploring what made them successful in the first place[6]. How did Nike, one of dozens of small brands with very limited financial resources, distribution and brand awareness, and no technological advantage, manage to become the number one brand? How did Nike succeed against competitors who had a multiple to spend on marketing, established distribution and brand advantages and sometimes also a technologically superior product?

How did Jack Daniels, one of a multitude of small US distilleries, with a laughable marketing budget, lack of distribution, low level of brand awareness and no financial resources to speak of become the number one US and, subsequently, one of the leading global whiskey brands?

How did Ben & Jerry's, one of hundreds of ambitious ice cream retailers, with no financial backing, a minute marketing budget, and a lack of distribution infra-

---

[6] Douglas Holt and Douglas Cameron, *Cultural Strategy: Using Innovative Ideologies to Build Breakthrough Brands*, Oxford University Press, 2010.

structure beat some much better funded competitors to become a leading ice cream chain?

Many more case studies can be found in Holt & Cameron's book, but I think you get the picture. But there is another reason for delving into Holt & Cameron's work: they demonstrate how a brand that is aligned with an emerging ideology during a time of cultural disruption can achieve success against all odds.

Some of the brand owners they discuss were no doubt simply lucky and found themselves in the right place at the right time (e.g., Nike, Jack Daniels). Others (such as Ben & Jerry's) intuitively understood the opportunities a cultural disruption offers, and others again (such as Marlboro) doggedly pursued an understanding of these opportunities that would eventually allow them to capitalize on them.

Given that we are now at the beginning of one of the most significant cultural disruptions since the middle of last century, it makes sense for marketers to give serious thought to the emerging ideologies that will undoubtedly arise over the next couple of decades due to technological disruption.

Importantly, all the brands Holt & Cameron discuss – or rather their custodians – were able to exploit a disruption opportunity once they caught on to it. How to identify and exploit such an opportunity is the central focus of Holt & Cameron's *Cultural Disruption*. You will find many world leading brands amongst those that have benefitted from such a disruption, but your journey needs to take you back to their beginnings because that's when the foundation to their success was laid.

For most marketers the lessons we can learn from these early stages are invaluable because, even though they don't have the budgets, distribution, sponsorship opportunities, advertising clout or product innovation pipeline that solidify the market positions of today's leading brands, they can still benefit dramatically from a cultural disruption opportunity.

The essence
The thinking underlying the cultural disruption concept is that your strategy is the most powerful and will give your brand a strong, long-term differentiation platform when it capitalizes on cultural disruption that is already taking place, regardless of what you do with your brand. So you can either ride the wave of disruption or you can just continue to struggle on, focusing on incremental progress.

Brand strategy typically looks at the market as comprising of *individual* purchasers or consumers of the goods or services offered. This is not to say that group and social elements are ignored, but they are typically only considered in light of how they impact on the perceptions, attitudes, preferences and decisions of individuals. Similarly, when more than one person is involved in making a purchase decision, the focus is typically on how these social factors impact on the decisions of individual consumers.

For example, we may acknowledge that many young people seek the approval of their peer group or that many men are influenced by what others think about their abilities and thus take these social influences into account, but we explore them with a focus on how they shape the attitudes, feelings and behavior of the individual consumer in our target group. In other words, conventional marketing treats social or cultural influences as factors that need to be explored and understood so we can gain a better understanding of the *individual* consumer.

To develop a cultural strategy, however, you need to take a different approach. The focus needs to be on cultural values, and the objective is to align your brand with these values. These cultural values are determined by a prevailing ideology that allows individuals to make sense of the world and their place in it.

If you accept that having a brand express the prevailing ideology is likely to lead to success, it immediately becomes obvious that there are opportunities and threats in times of ideological disruption, that is, when a prevailing ideology loses significance and people are looking for a new, emerging ideology to replace it. When this happens, your focus needs to shift to identifying the latent demand for ideology and satisfying this demand, rather than building your strategy on your understanding of how individual consumers make their purchase decisions.

Take, for example, a time when Americans became increasingly dissatisfied with the idea of the corporate man and what Holt and Cameron call the 'white collar sweat-shop'. By recognizing this dissatisfaction and presenting new cultural values, Corona managed to replace Heineken as the leading imported beer brand in the United States. Corona presented a cultural expression that resonated with the ideological needs of their target audience, which they symbolized by showing people relaxing on a Mexican beach with a Corona – doing nothing.

The opportunity is typically greatest when there is historical change - a social disruption that shakes up the category's cultural conventions such as a realization that the white-collar sweat-shop was not really offering Americans the life they aspired to.

The key pieces of the Cultural Disruption puzzle
Unfortunately, the terminology used by Holt and Cameron is not consistent with that of neuroscience or neurobranding. With apologies to Holt & Cameron, I have adapted it to bring it into line with the terminology used elsewhere.

Cultural codes[7]
Holt and Cameron suggest that cultural codes provide us with markers on our life journey. They help us to understand the world we live in and our place in this world. They form the basis of our value judgments. Different societies typically have quite different values,

---

[7] Holt and Cameron use the term 'cultural expressions.'

which are also evident in their respective cultural expressions. Today, mass media and commerce are important and powerful forces that shape cultural codes, and brands can be highly effective when they are on-code.

Ideology, myth and cultural signals[8]
Let's move from this conceptual view to the specific, operational elements. According to Holt and Cameron, cultural codes are composed of ideology, myth, and cultural signals.

An *ideology* is a belief system that is shared by a group of people. Ideologies shape how we see the world, how we judge others, and how we act ourselves. Brands can present a particular point of view on a cultural construct that is central to the product, such as beer or cigarettes 'commenting' on the nature of masculinity.

Ideologies change over time, and this opens up opportunities for a brand to disrupt by aligning itself with a new, emerging ideology. For example, an ideology related to masculinity may at one stage be based on the 'corporate man' who drives America's progress, and at another time on self-reliant working-class frontier masculinity (as expressed by the Jack Daniels and Marlboro brands). Clearly, brands that express a particular ideology depend for their success on this being the prevalent ideology amongst their target customers.

Ideology can, of course, be expressed in any number of ways. The important point is that, while we can explain an ideology rationally, it comes alive through *qualitative myths and cultural signals.*

Holt and Cameron define myths as 'instructive stories that impart ideologies' and suggest that *"to resonate with consumers, [a myth] must be composed using the most appropriate and compelling cultural content - cultural*

---

[8] Holt and Cameron use the term 'cultural codes.'

[signals]."[9]

Importantly, all mass cultural signals, including those in advertising and marketing communications in general, rely on elements for which the meaning has been well established in the past. It is this established meaning that allows cultural signals to work like shorthand for consumers, allowing them to understand and experience the intended meanings. Think about the Marlboro Man on a horse and how he is dressed, what he does, the environment he is in, and so on. These signals collectively create the intended meaning.

In summary, *"cultural innovations break through when they bear the right ideology, which is dramatized through the right myth, expressed with the right cultural [signals]."*[10]

Subcultures are particularly important as they give credibility to the cultural innovation by demonstrating that the ideology already exists, at least within a subculture. This means that we are not presenting an idea that is essentially utopian in nature, but rather pointing to a subculture that has already adopted the ideology we present and suggesting it is relevant to a much larger group of people. For example Nike showed how African-American athletes who came from disadvantaged backgrounds succeeded against all odds. Later the brand focused on women who were not given the same opportunities that were open to men, yet still succeeded. This was aligned with the cultural disruption taking place in the US at the time, when many Americans feared that their country had lost its economic leadership position to Japan. Or consider Jack Daniels telling stories about life in Kentucky where time is not an issue, presenting an alternative to the harassed American manager.

The subculture makes your myth tangible and gives it substance. It also allows those exposed to your communications to pick up the cultural signals you are using. In other words, it provides the broader context

---

[9] ibid., p.175
[10] ibid., p 176

within which these cultural signals become meaningful, complementary elements.

The process
Holt and Cameron refer to the six stage model but are quick to point out that these are not six consecutive stages. Rather, each stage might provide new insights and perspectives that lead you back to an earlier stage to review the material you gathered at that point in time and the conclusions you have drawn from it.

Once you have developed a cultural strategy and get feedback from the market place you may want to adapt or aggressively revise your strategy in light of these learnings. Early feedback is essential as it allows you to understand where you have captured a new ideology you are aligning your brand with, and where you have failed to do so. It is not uncommon for the early strategy to go through significant adaptations before it delivers the dramatic impact you are seeking.

While flexibility and refinement are important, it is nevertheless useful to familiarize yourself with Holt and Cameron's six stage model because it brings together the key pieces of the puzzle and provides you with some structure when you embark on your cultural disruption journey.

(1) Map the category's cultural orthodoxy
To start with you need to understand the conventional cultural expression that is typical for your industry sector. A review of marketing activities and collateral across competitors should allow you to identify the ideology, myth and cultural code.

You are looking to identify the common themes, symbols, product features, retail channels and so forth that can be found in most marketing activities, including new product development, product and package design, marketing communications, brand activation, shopper marketing initiatives and so forth.

If you can't identify these cultural conventions you won't

be able to see how they can be disrupted, so this first step is crucial and you should be prepared to spend some time and effort on exploring and mapping the category's cultural orthodoxy.

Here are some questions that may help:
- How do brands (in your category) talk to consumers? Do they talk down to them, or are they having a friendly conversation? Are they down to earth, or quite removed from real life and aspirational?
- Who is representing these brands? A celebrity? A person of authority (such as a medical practitioner)? An average person?
- What or who is giving these brands credibility?
- What is portrayed as essential or at least desirable (e.g., the whole family having a meal together, eating a good breakfast to get through the day, using products that make you get noticed; etc.)?
- What are the typical contexts in which these brands are shown (e.g., mother in the kitchen, kids around the breakfast table, a car driving on open road, etc.)?

(2) Identify the social disruption that can dislodge the orthodoxy

During times of social shifts you may find that consumers no longer identify with conventional category expressions. These disruptive social shifts can be led by technological, economic, social, demographic or other developments, and may be championed by mass media or social movements. These factors disrupt consumers' identification with conventional category expressions.

Ask yourself what has changed or is changing. For example:
- Are there any dramatic changes in the way people feel about their life or aspects of their life?
- Are there dramatic shifts in lifestyle due to technology or other factors?
- Are there generational shifts?
- Are there significant changes in how people do what they do (e.g., because of advances in technology)?
- Is the social fabric collapsing, perhaps because of a

recession or large-scale political changes?

(3) Unearth the ideological opportunity

Once you have specified the social disruption you need to identify consumers' collective desires and anxieties in relation to this disruption.

Questions to ask include:
- Do people feel insecure because of changes in their work or private life, because of changes in opportunities (e.g., rising unemployment, credit harder to get)?
- Do people feel confused because life no longer follows the same largely predictable path as before?
- Is there an emerging 'enemy', that is, are people opposing a political direction, big business, the growth of the welfare state, their elected leaders, immigrants, et cetera?
- How did the now-disappearing ideology help consumers to make sense of their world in the past?
- What were the essential expectations consumers had while they held on to this ideology?
- What has changed, or what do consumers fear will change, that creates confusion or anxiety?

(4) Gather appropriate source material

Cultural innovations repurpose cultural expressions we can find in subcultures, social movements, media myths, and the brand's own assets. Holt and Cameron call this source material. It is important to stress that this is not about ideas but rather about finding a group of people that has already adopted a new ideology and thus proves that the new ideology is not just an idea but can be successfully subscribed to. The ideological opportunity usually provides the focus for this search. Sometimes the business is embedded in a movement or subculture that is relevant (e.g., Jack Daniels or Nike).

Questions you should ask include:
- Are there any subcultures that already embody the new, emerging ideology?
- Is your business embedded in a subculture that could

give credibility to the new ideology?

(5) Can you apply cultural tactics?

Holt and Cameron stress that it is not always possible or desirable to apply tactics. However, it is worthwhile to consider this option. They suggest six tactics for your review:

- *Provoking ideological flashpoints* - political, societal or cultural issues that attract a lot of attention.
- *Mythologizing the company* - look at the history, the founder, what made the company or brand great.
- *Resuscitating reactionary ideology* - align with an ideology that is contrary to the current ideology, but only if the current one is crumbling.
- *Cultural capital trickle-down* - link into cultural behavior that is manifesting itself, such as taking a vitamin pill a day.
- *Crossing the cultural chasm* - be the brand that makes it possible to cross the cultural chasm between where we are and where we want to be, like Starbucks offering a 'third place' to spend time in.
- *Cultural Jujitsu* - focus on a major opponent and enter into battle, positioning yourself as David facing Goliath, while provoking your opponent to attack you.

(6) Craft the cultural strategy

Holt and Cameron suggest that *"cultural strategy requires identifying a specific opportunity that opens up at a particular historical moment, within a particular societal context; and then responding to that opportunity with a particular cultural expression, made up of ideology, myth, and cultural codes"*.

It follows from all this that the way a cultural strategy is developed is quite different to an ideas-driven or market research-driven brand strategy. It is also clear that a cultural strategy needs to be very clear about the cultural disruption that has been identified and the strategy that will align the brand with a new, emerging ideology. Last but not least, the signals the brand sends at all touchpoints must be aligned with this cultural strategy.

To achieve this you need to develop a detailed blue-print rather than the usual superficial template used for documenting brand strategies and plans. Questions may include:

- Is there a logical, simple way forward resulting from the disruption which may be difficult to follow, but is easy to understand (e.g. *'we have to become tougher and more productive'*)?
- What new ideology would fit the emerging new world and would lessen confusion and anxiety?
- What is the emergent ideology that customers are gravitating towards?
- In what way could your brand be a champion when it comes to bringing this new ideology to life?
- Could your brand represent, create or tap into a subculture that is already providing proof that it is possible to adopt this ideology?
- How could your brand gain credibility in providing or being aligned with the emerging new ideology?

Times of opportunity
As Holt and Cameron note, *"at some point, as history unfolds and social structures shift, one or more of these shifts will be disruptive, challenging the taken-for-granted cultural [codes] offered by category incumbents, and creating emergent demand for new cultural [codes]. This is what we call a social disruption. These are moments when once-dominant brands lose their resonance and when innovative brands take off because they deliver the right [signals]."* [11]

Cultural disruptions create ideological opportunities. The category's orthodoxy no longer adequately delivers the cultural code consumers demand. Consumers look for brands that champion new ideologies, brought to life by new myths and cultural signals.

Clearly, today we are at the beginning of a cultural revolution that will change the way most of us live. Technologies will replace humans, with a large – and

---
[11] ibid., p. 185

increasing – number of people finding themselves out of work. Meanwhile inequality is increasing and will increase even more given that a small number of companies have a huge share of the market for key technologies or a dominant position with respect to market access.

In many developed countries consumers have got used to growth, punctuated only temporarily by an economic crisis. The most recent Global Financial Crisis was more than just a brief disruption, but even so it is nothing compared to what lies ahead. In many developing countries, meanwhile, progress has been made with lifting hundreds of millions out of poverty.

Early on, technologies replacing workers will have the most significant impact on developing countries as outsourcing manufacturing to such countries is not an attractive option when Artificial Intelligence and robotics facilitate low-cost manufacturing and service delivery. In the next wave it will eliminate a significant percentage of jobs in the developed world.

No doubt we all will have to look for ideologies that are not built around deriving our sense of personal worth from work, income and assets, growth and competition. Fertile ground indeed for any brand that wants to benefit from cultural disruption.

However, a warning is in order: To develop a cultural strategy is a challenging task, and many of the case examples presented by Holt and Cameron suggest that it often takes a company and its agency partners several years to finally get the formula right. Therefore, this is not something you should embark on when you are developing a campaign under severe time pressure. To my mind, it represents a long-term investment that can potentially deliver much greater returns than a conventional marketing approach but it will take time and patience and, most of all, it will require you to let go of conventional marketing practices.

The biggest challenge is to bring the various elements

of your strategy together in a way that presents the ideological opportunity in a compelling and original manner. And when it comes to implementing your strategy you have to make sure that you send engaging, high-impact signals that are on-code at each key touchpoint where your target group 'meets' your brand.

For more information you should read Douglas Holt's earlier book *How Brands Become Icons: The Principles of Cultural Branding* (2004) and the book he co-authored with Douglas Cameron some years later *Cultural Strategy: Using Innovative Ideologies to Build Breakthrough Brands* (2012).

8.3 Radically innovating what things mean

Roberto Verganti suggests that consumer-centric market research is bound to come up with only incremental improvements that may well not deliver the sales boost the company is seeking. He has a valid point: consider that some 85 per cent of new products fail, and the majority of them have been researched and launched because consumers said they would buy them once they become available. There is also ample evidence that products consumers rejected in market research went on to become significant successes, such as the Aeron chair, the Beogram 4000 B&O system, Bailey's Irish Cream, the Walkman and ATM machines.

But what's the alternative?

If you want to experience a consistent flow of big, innovative concepts and strategies you have to first change the framework you are thinking within. As long as you stick with the conventional way of looking at your products and brands you are unlikely to come up with ground-breaking new solutions to the marketing challenges you face. But once you have a dramatic change in perspective (i.e., you see your brands, their positioning and the market place differently to the way your competitors do), you can tap into a huge reservoir of disruptive concepts and strategies that will last you for a very long time.

Verganti[12] presents a sound methodology you can follow to change your perspective and identify high-impact concepts and strategies. While he is an academic (with the Milano Politecnico) he has barrow-loads of practical experience gained in working with some of Europe's most progressive companies. But let me say up front, his approach is fundamental in nature: not a little project on the side or a tweaking of mainstream marketing

---

[12] Roberto Verganti, *Design-Driven Innovation. Changing the Rules of Competition by Radically Innovating What Things Mean*, Harvard Business Press, 2009.

processes and practices, but a fundamental shift in how you innovate. I have no doubt that this approach provides a sound platform for on-going innovation, but it is not a quick fix.

Verganti proposes that companies can change the rules of competition by radically *innovating what things mean*.[13] McDonalds has changed the meaning of fast food, Verganti argues, and Intuit's Quickbooks – designed for business users who hate accounting – changed the meaning of accounting software. Alessi has, for many years, pursued radical innovation in what household objects could mean to people. Meanwhile, Swatch changed the meaning of watches, and Big Brother changed the meaning of a TV show by introducing reality TV.

You know all that, of course, but what Verganti offers is a systematic approach to coming up with radical innovations that change what products mean. Here are some of the key principles:

For a start, *forget user-centric innovation*. There is no point in asking consumers what they want, because they are set in the way they perceive products and brands. Market research leads to incremental thinking, which in turn results in incremental improvements rather than radical innovation.

Leading companies, Verganti assures us, are not driven by market research. Verganti relates how a marketing manager for Apple once described its market research as consisting of *'Steve looking in the mirror every morning and asking himself what he wanted'.*

Verganti came to the conclusion that there are three innovation strategies:
- *market pull-based strategies* that are user-centered – these typically lead to only incremental improvements and don't generate new meanings

---
[13] In a later section I will extend Verganti's concept from things (i.e., products) to brands.

- *technology push strategies* that lead to radical improvements and may or may not generate new meanings (e.g., the Wii used a new chip, the accelerator chip, that facilitates the games offered)
- *design-driven (design push) strategies* that generate new meanings (e.g, Alessi, Swatch).

Verganti notes that sometimes technological change underlies a design-driven strategy, resulting in a mixed technology push/design-driven strategy. For example, Nintendo's Wii strategy was based on using accelerometers that allow the console to sense the speed and orientation of the controller. While the technological innovation facilitated the resulting product, it was the design that created new meaning, i.e., a computer game that was a totally different kind of 'game', offering new benefits and attracting a new market.

How to embark on design-driven innovation
To illustrate the key steps I will use *Artemide,* an Italian light manufacturer that elevated strategic thinking from functional aspects (*How can I make my next-generation lighting products more effective?*) or aesthetics (*What should the next-generation floor lamps look like?*) to the essential benefits of light. This led to the realization that light can affect mood, which in turn led to the development of the *Metamorfosi* range of light products, designed not only to provide light but to affect people's mood:

First, look at a particular aspect or *slice of life* rather than at the narrow use of a product (e.g., focusing on people coming home tired at night rather than on the users of lamps).

Second, rather than just focusing on a 'user,' focus on *a person*, with all the complexity that brings: How does this person feel? What is important to this person at that time? How would this person like to feel? What does this person do at this time? and so forth. This allows you to broaden the set of goals you could potentially address, such as the consumer wanting to feel comforted and relaxed rather than hassled and exhausted.

Third, recognize that you are focusing on a person in a *life context that is of great relevance to other manufacturers and service providers* (in this example, this might include manufacturers of furniture, personal computers, game consoles, smart-system developers, and media broadcasters). All of these interested parties pursue an understanding of how people could give meaning to things in their homes, and they may be willing to share that knowledge.

Importantly, there are not just competitors aiming at the same slice of life and person, but also organizations offering complementary services. A food manufacturer, for example, may ask themselves how the person preparing the food feels, what meaning the food and the act of preparing it has, what emotions they feel, how success or failure manifests itself, and so on.

This slice of life (preparing food) and person (who prepares the food) is also the focus of kitchen designers and manufacturers; grocery retailers and manufacturers of grocery brands; white goods, kitchen utensils or equipment manufacturers; glassware and crockery suppliers; TV broadcasters and other media organizations that develop and deliver cooking-related content; online services focusing on recipes, cooking, health aspects of different foods; public servants who aim at educating the public about the food they should eat; as well as ethnographers who explore the role of food and food preparation, sociologists, neuroscientists, and so forth.

Because these parties have complementary goals and perspectives, they are likely to look not only at different aspects of this slice of life, but they also look at it differently. This means that sharing insights and perspectives will allow all parties to gain a much deeper and useful understanding of this slice of life and the person at the center of attention. It follows that a key element of developing strategies that change the meaning of things is to build a network of parties that have the same interest in the slice of life you have, but have different perspectives because they offer complementary products and services.

Clearly, the ability of your firm to attract and engage these parties – Veganti calls them 'interpreters' – is a critical success factor. Importantly, the interaction with interpreters tends to continue over long periods of time, sometimes several years.

Extending the scope of Verganti's approach to brands
As Verganti's focus is on design, he limits his observations to products and doesn't include brands in his assessment. But can a repositioning of brands lead to a change in the meaning of things without resorting to product development?

This is not an idle question, as research has demonstrated that brands can have a significant impact on the consumer's experience by adding value and, importantly, by creating qualities that may allow the consumer to address their goals. The very same product may not be able to do the same if it were unbranded or carried a different brand.

This is the same principle as the familiar 'placebo effect' often found in studies on the efficacy of pharmaceutical drugs.

For example[14], headaches can start to subside as soon as a headache tablet has been taken and long before the medication could have possibly taken effect. The act of taking a headache tablet is the trigger that leads the brain to reduce the level of pain. More bizarrely, an experiment that used placebo chemotherapy for cancer found that

---

[14] I have collected these from various sources, including: Genco, Steven, Andrew Pohlmann, Peter Steidl, *Neuromarketing for Dummies*, Wiley 2013; Peter Steidl, *Neurobranding*, Create Space 2012; Scheier, Christian and Dirk Held, *Wie Werbung Wirkt. Erkenntnisse des Neuromarketing*, Haufe 2010; Scheier Christian, Dirk Bayas-Linke and Johannes Schneider, *Codes. Die geheime Sprache der Produkte*, Haufe 2010; A.K. Pradeep, *The Buying Brain. Secrets for selling to the subconscious mind*, Wiley 2010

30% of the patients experienced sickness and lost hair, neither of which could have been caused by the placebo drug.

More interesting from our point of view is an experiment where subjects received Aspirin in an Aspirin pack, a placebo in an Aspirin pack, Aspirin in an unbranded pack and, finally, a placebo in an unbranded pack. The branded placebo worked significantly better than the placebo with no brand. The unbranded Aspirin worked better than the branded placebo but not as well as the branded Aspirin.

A multitude of experiments have also been conducted in which consumers are given a well-known and established brand-name product in unmarked packaging or disguised as an inferior brand. Invariably, consumers believe the product presented under its established brand performs better than the same product when it is offered to them under the inferior brand's packaging.

In marketing we refer to this as priming, because the brand primes the consumption experience. But we can also look at this as a placebo effect: in reality, the brand has nothing to do with the product's performance, yet the presence or absence of the brand can have a significant impact on how the offer is experienced.

What we have demonstrated so far is that brands can have a determining impact on the consumption experience. This would suggest that if we change the meaning of a brand we might also change the meaning of the products offered under this brand.

So much for the theory. Is there any evidence in practice?

Bottled water is a good example: repositioning bottled water brands as superior, even exclusive brands has changed the meaning of water. Who would have thought that something in abundance in many markets and available at a cost that is too small to even measure when it comes to a mere bottle of it, would end up as a conspicuous consumption opportunity costing up to $30 per bottle? But these days the brand of bottled water you serve at your dinner party may say as much about you as the food.

There is, however, a caveat. Simply positioning a brand as prestigious, lifting the price and bringing the packaging into line with the new positioning rarely leads to a change in meaning. For example, positioning a wine as a premium wine does not change the meaning of 'wine'.

Water is different because for many people it was a functional item – a necessity one gave little thought to – that was freely available at a miniscule cost. Bottled water changed the meaning of water just like the Swatch changed the meaning of watches. You still drink it, just like you still check the time on your Swatch – but the meaning has moved from a functional one (time keeping or rehydration) to an emotional one (fashion or prestige).

Again, not every repositioning of a brand changes the meaning of the brand. It may change the attributes one associates with the brand, it may change the usage or consumption occasion, it may change how much consumers are prepared to pay for the brand – but the meaning of the brand may remain the same.

When it comes to retail, we may not change the physical offering as much as the way it is presented. Take Sephora, a chain offering cosmetic products arranged by type of product rather than by brand, creating a totally different shopping environment that encourages comparisons across brands, at the same creating its own style rather than the usual retail setup where each of the major cosmetics brands has its allocated counter designed in a way that expresses their own style. At Sephora, you can browse across brands and appreciate the wide range within each category. This may sound like a small change, but in reality it has created a store atmosphere and functional environment that disrupts the industry standard.

In summary, it is a fine line we are treading here between what does and does not constitute 'new meaning' when it comes to brands. Fortunately, this is not an academic treatise, but a practical assessment of disruptive opportunities. This leaves room for your own personal interpretation which may be rather narrow or very broad when it comes to deciding what is - and is not – likely to change the meaning of your brand.

One observation may be helpful here: in many categories the meaning of the category has changed over time. Many food categories have changed from being purely functional to addressing a range of health and wellness issues (e.g., fortified dairy products); dishwashers have moved from being positioned as a prestige item to a functional item that saves time and then to a healthier way to clear dishes and avoid bacteria; gyms have changed from delivering fitness to offering a lifestyle choice; breakfast cereals have changed from an inexpensive food that fills the kids up to a healthy choice that provides children with the energy they need to get through the day.

In many cases there was an early trail-blazer, a brand that changed the meaning of the offer made. But over time other brands followed and eventually the meaning of the whole category changed.

Organizational requirements
Verganti presents detailed case examples that demonstrate how this process unfolds. His argument is compelling, yet it is clear that to adopt what he calls design-driven innovation requires an organizational culture characterized by a willingness to:
- explore and think widely
- share insights and results with other, non-competing, parties that share the same interest
- lift the exploration from a narrow product focus to the context of a person's life where the product (may) have meaning
- take a long rather than short-term view
- and, finally, be prepared to disrupt by changing the meaning of products, services and, ultimately, brands.

This list of success criteria unfortunately excludes most

companies, because a short-term focus and an emphasis on incremental improvements are rampant in most firms.

For more information and case examples read Roberto Verganti, *Design-Driven Innovation. Changing the Rules of Competition by Radically Innovating What Things Mean* (2009).

8.4 Developing a higher-level emotional relationship

You could position your brand not on the basis of your offer (product quality, product features and innovations, packaging, price, distribution channels, terms of purchase, etc.), but rather move the brand positioning to a higher emotional level. That is, position the brand as not just addressing the typical category-related goals, but also more important emotional goals the category has not addressed in the past.

For this to occur, the engagement with the consumer has to happen with an aspect that is not part of your – or your competitors' – traditional marketing mix. That is, you have to elevate a conventional marketing strategy to something the consumer values more than your product offer.

This is not a new strategy, but neuroscience has allowed us to understand how and why this strategy works with habitually bought brands and this should, in turn, allow you to achieve a better hit rate. Think about Dove's '*Natural Beauty,*' Nike's '*Just Do It!*', Apple's relentless focus on innovation or, to add an older example, Pedigree's '*We're For Dogs*'.

In these and other cases, the marketing didn't focus on product features, price, package variations or other aspects that might encourage the consumer to start comparing the offer with that of competitive brands. Rather, it focused the consumer's attention on the brand's particular values or the interests and commitments they shared with consumers, thus setting the brand apart from its competitors.

It is easy for competitors to copy discounts or imitate product innovation and package variations. It is difficult, if not impossible, for them to copy campaigns that operate at the level of higher values. There are four main reasons for this:
- There are legal limitations under passing-off legislation.

- Consumers are not likely to look favorably on a competitor that is clearly just copying a positioning the consumer values highly. In such a case, the consumer would be more likely to reward the 'original'.
- It takes time and effort to find an acceptable variation to the strategic position taken by a brand that has built a strong, disruptive positioning based on higher values.
- There is something like a code of ethics in most markets that would discourage agencies and their clients from simply copying a grand strategy.

I will use the old Maslow's Hierarchy of Needs concept to illustrate this strategy – not because the consumer's mind is neatly organized in this way, but because it provides a simple framework to illustrate where the emotional relationship between a brand and the consumer resides.

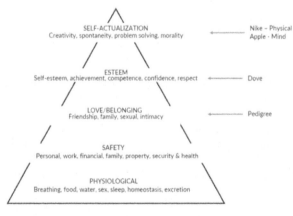

Illustration 12: *Hierarchy of needs*

For example:
- Dove's *Real Beauty* aims at lifting the relationship with the brand to the level of *self-esteem* showing that the brand understands the consumer and is helping her to gain self-esteem.
- Nike's *Just Do It!* lifted the relationship to the *self-actualization* level – focusing on the physical rather than the mental side, with the latter being Apple's focus.
- Pedigree developed a higher-level emotional relationship with the '*We're for Dogs*' campaign that did not focus on product features but on dogs, taking the relationship with consumers to the level of *love/belonging*.

It would, however, be a grave mistake to assume that all a brand needs to do is to claim that it champions some cause or other. Things are not that simple and evidence is also necessary. Pedigree – the brand that claims '*We're for Dogs*' – sponsors dog adoption programs, while Dove runs self-esteem workshops for girls. Nike stages the Nike Run as just one of its initiatives. Apple is a bit of an aberration as it uses its products to confirm that is doesn't just talk about innovation and creativity but actually delivers on this front.

Dove

Dove's '*Real Beauty*' strategy moves the brand from competing at the product or price level to the *esteem* level by emphasizing that natural beauty should be celebrated, not the artificial beauty of photo-shopped, hungry-looking models usually seen in magazines, fashion shows and advertising. Dove is positioned as a Champion brand that aims at taking the pressure off women who feel inadequate if they don't look like fashion models.

This repositioning saw Dove move from a brand that offered a range of products to a brand that truly understands the consumer, thus becoming the consumer's Champion for natural beauty. Of course, this only works when carried right through, and in

Dove's case the most visible and obvious way of bringing this positioning alive was with the use of 'normal' women of all sizes and shapes in the Dove advertisements. But Dove has gone even further than this, including starting the Dove Self Esteem Fund for girls in a number of markets and by conducting self-esteem workshops for girls.

It should be obvious that this strategy will encourage women who feel strongly about this issue to develop respect – and possibly a preference – for Dove. An important point is that this strategy is also likely to work with habitual buyers. Let's hypothesize how a habitual Dove buyer and a habitual buyer of a competitive brand might respond to the Dove *'Real Beauty'* campaign. Assuming the values embodied by the campaign resonate (i.e., align with a goal the consumer has), the habitual Dove buyer would endorse the campaign and feel very happy that she regularly buys Dove. The campaign does not encourage any comparisons at the product or price level. The consumer is likely to continue to buy Dove habitually, except while the campaign is still a strong memory she may smile and feel good when putting Dove into her shopping trolley.

The non-habitual Dove buyer may also notice and be touched by the campaign and wonder if she shouldn't buy a brand that really understands her, given that the brand she usually buys doesn't seem to care about these values. For many shoppers, existing habits that drive them to purchase a competitive brand will be stronger than the campaign's impact, but some will change to Dove, leading to an increase in market share. Mission accomplished!

Pedigree
The principles are the same, so I will keep this short. At a time when dog food brands were primarily competing at the product level by offering additional vitamins or minerals, larger chunks, or flavors and textures that dogs prefer, Pedigree launched the *'We're for Dogs'* campaign, a very simple proposition packaged up in a beautiful and

often touching campaign.

Later extensions delivered a program that aimed at getting homeless dogs adopted, refreshing the positioning and giving it new credibility. In this case, Pedigree lifted the brand from competing at the product level to competing at the level of *'love and belonging*,' as shown in Maslow's pyramid.

And again, we can see how this campaign didn't upset the habitual buying of existing customers, as they were not encouraged to focus on a product feature that a competitor would be able to lay claim to as well (or even outperform on). Rather, they were reinforced in their habitual buying by feeling that Pedigree shares a core value with them: a love of dogs.

At the same time, there were plenty of habitual buyers of competing brands that migrated to Pedigree, as evidenced by the market share gains the brand could book.

I have presented case examples to illustrate how the relationship between a brand and the consumer can be taken to a higher value level, i.e. positioned in line with a goal the consumer sees as more important that the functional product benefits. I should add that the product benefits still have to be delivered, regardless. A consumer is unlikely to buy a product that is deficient simply because it addresses a higher level goal. However, given that many brands enjoy parity with respect to product performance, and the likelihood that consumers are unable or unwilling to undertake a detailed assessment of these benefits, the consumer is likely to respond well to a brand that addresses a higher-level value.

To take the brand into higher-level territory it can own, you have to address a number of requirements:
- Firstly, the brand needs to stand for a purpose or mission that resonates emotionally with the consumer, that is, it addresses a higher-level emotional goal.
- Second, you need to convince the consumer that your

brand can address this higher level goal and deliver the emotions the consumer is seeking.
- Third, you need to create a strong, tangible link between the higher-level purpose or value and the brand, i.e., walk the talk.

As always, the consumer's goals will ultimately determine your success. You will recall that the Dove campaign did not work at all in Russia and China where many consumers wanted to look like models and did not feel under pressure by the depiction of women in the media and existing advertising.

Turbo-charging your strategy: encouraging the development of Brand Tribes

When creating a higher-level emotional relationship between the consumer and the brand it is often the brand that feeds this relationship. With a Brand Tribe consumers add to the excitement they feel about the brand by interacting with each other and reinforcing their mutual feeling about the brand.

Of course, these are not mutually exclusive strategies – you can develop an emotional relationship at a higher level and then create a Brand Tribe to turbocharge your brand's progress. But first things first: What exactly is a Brand Tribe?

To capture the essence of a Brand Tribe consider the different types of relationships consumers may have with your brand and with each other. Some consumers will regularly buy your brand but they won't have a strong emotional relationship with the brand. Their purchase behavior is largely driven instead by simple habit, or price, convenience, availability or other factors. These consumers are clearly not members of a Brand Tribe.

Others may feel strongly about your brand and have a true brand preference. They may even admire your brand and recommend it to others. They may participate in engagement opportunities you offer them, such as competitions and events. But they do not have any interest in others who also 'follow' the brand – they have a *one-on-one relationship with your brand.* One-on-one relationships are very different to the relationships that define a Brand Tribe.

Finally, there may be consumers who feel very strongly about your brand *and* who feel a close tie to other consumers who have the same kind of relationship with the brand. They *engage with other consumers* who follow the brand, the common bond being their admiration of, interest in, or at least strong preference for, that brand. These consumers belong to a Brand Tribe.

In summary, when I talk about a Brand Tribe I am referring to *a group of consumers or followers who share a strong commitment to the brand, which manifests itself in engaging with each other with the brand being the catalyst or focus of this engagement.*

A clear indicator of this engagement is the sharing of content. However, when it comes to sharing there are active and passive sharers, just as in sports there are active and passive participants. Some perform and others simply look on – but without the performers they would obviously have nothing to look at!

The same applies to Brand Tribes: some parties share and respond to content shared by others (active tribe members), while others consume the content that is being generated but they don't actively participate (passive tribe members). Typically, the passive group is larger – often by a significant margin – than the active group. But which is more important? Clearly, those who actively share content, as without them the passive group would lose the very foundation of their engagement with other members of the tribe. It follows that *the key to building a Brand Tribe is to build strong engagement with the brand and to get consumers to share content.*

If sharing is central to building or maintaining a Brand Tribe it is important to understand the benefits consumers can derive from sharing content. And, to understand these benefits I need to explore what happens in the brain because it is, after all, our brain that determines what we do.[15]

When you address a goal you get a dopamine release. It follows that you get a dopamine hit when you share content if you are expecting (or at least hoping) to generate some kind of reaction – get a view, a response, a like, be acknowledged in some way. Sharing might make you feel important; help you to position yourself as funny, cool, or knowledgeable; or it may simply confirm in your mind that you belong. In other words, you are addressing a goal.[16]

Importantly, when you expose consumers to a message (such as an ad or an engagement opportunity) that is aligned with the content they recently shared, you will find these consumers far more receptive to your message than others who have not shared. This is because the dopamine level decreases with time after the consumer has shared content. When your message arrives, and it is aligned with the way a dopamine release was triggered not long ago through sharing, the brain sees this as an opportunity to repeat the dopamine hit. This explains the power of re-targeting. (I explain this more fully in the chapter on marketing communications.)

What makes a group of consumers a Brand Tribe is not the formal step of joining a membership or loyalty scheme, a social media group or some other kind of community. Rather, the criterion is how people *feel* about others who share their positive perception of the brand, and the most reliable indicator of who does and doesn't

---

[15] *Dopamine and the science of social media sharing*, Peter Steidl, WARC Exclusive, August 2016. This article explores the neuroscience behind social sharing and how brands can better understand dopamine cycles to make social media content more engaging, including programmatic and effective targeting techniques.

[16] I am ignoring sharing content as an obligation that does not address a goal and is bare of any emotional involvement, such as sending a client a brochure she asked for or sending your accountant some information on transactions.

belong to a Brand Tribe is arguably the sharing of content.

Members of a tribe have a strong emotional commitment and will keep following the brand even if it doesn't perform (such as a football club that is on a long losing streak or a brand that is mature and boring). They will keep following because *they still get dopamine hits from relating to other members.* Rather than talking about some amazing things the brand does today they may reminisce about the golden past, or they may share ideas about exciting new things the brand could do (e.g., a leading energy drink attracts spontaneous suggestions for new ads and initiatives from its Brand Tribe). The point is that Brand Tribe members can still gain emotional benefits and therefore dopamine hits even if the brand does not excel.

Someone who has formally joined a tribe but does not emotionally engage with other members will drift away when the brand (or sports team) does not perform, as their only benefit was to see the brand excel. It follows that it is important for marketers to convert any mere followers into tribe members who interact, share and thus create dopamine hits.

Obviously, there are different ways of creating a Brand Tribe. Here I am simply taking the key elements that define a Brand Tribe to explore how these can be created or managed. These are:

Creating an emotional relationship between the brand and the consumer
A tribe typically does not form around a brand that lacks legitimacy. It seems more than acceptable for an athletic wear brand to encourage us to push our own physical boundaries or a dog food brand to express its love of dogs. But a brand that has no legitimacy – say a carbonated cola drink positioning itself as doing good (such as Pepsi tried to do with its Pepsi Challenge) – may struggle to build a Brand Tribe.

Adding engagement amongst consumers to a one-on-one relationship with the brand

The following strategies can help to create a stronger feeling of being part of a tribe:

Creating a common enemy

It is helpful to define the Brand Tribe, and the most effective way of doing this is to contrast the brand or the championed cause by highlighting who is the '*enemy*' because they don't support the values that represent the glue that holds the Tribe together.

Apple did this very effectively from the start, when it was just a computer brand. Of course Apple computers were different, but they were nevertheless just a different type of PC. Yet Apple understood that it would need to differentiate in absolute terms if it did not want to go the way of other small computer brands. So it created the idea that a computer can be an Apple *or* a PC or, said differently, that Apple is something very different to a PC. This created a common enemy – PCs and their owners – that Apple occasionally made fun of.

Dove created an enemy in the cosmetics industry and what it stands for. Nike focused on the enemy within – the forces that hold you back when it comes to realizing your potential. An obvious example for how effective a common enemy can be is a sports- related Brand Tribe such as a football club. Members of sporting associations or clubs see their chosen team as the one that is fighting off all other contenders. The common enemy is a key factor in keeping the Tribe together.

Striving for uniqueness

More and more brands are keen to establish a Brand Tribe. They typically attempt to broaden the scope of the territory they occupy to attract consumers and convert them to tribe membership. Differentiation and effective 'recruitment' of consumers into the Brand Tribe is already critically important, and will become even more so.

For example, companies from such diverse sectors as

health insurance, finance, health sciences, food and beverage, travel, self-monitoring gadgets, fitness centers, sports and leisure, and even entertainment are trying to build Brand Tribes around wellbeing and healthy lifestyle, encouraging engagement and generally attempting to become thought leaders in this field. No doubt there are plenty of consumers who might engage, but they are likely to end up becoming part of just one Brand Tribe.

Creating sub-tribes
Obviously, it is much easier to get interaction when we create smaller 'sub-tribes' that are more intimate and designed to benefit a smaller, often local, group. This is a common feature of professional associations that establish special interest or area chapters. Alcoholics Anonymous encourages members to attend meetings in whatever country or city they find themselves in, which means that they are not only a member of a sub-tribe, i.e., their regular group, but can also temporarily join other sub-tribes.

Humanization of the brand
Another, not uncommon option is to personify the brand by featuring individuals. For example, the Red Bull Air Race provides extensive information on its team members, encouraging consumers to follow a team member of their choice.

Summary
The vital point about Brand Tribes is that they typically address more than one goal when members share content. Brand Tribes reinforce a sense of belonging, and members may see sharing as an opportunity to compete for status (men especially), they may be able to explore something new or interesting by getting involved with other members of the tribe and, of course, all the while they can share and get a dopamine release from expecting to elicit a response or receive some other sort of positive feedback.

While sharing as such provides a dopamine release, you

can boost this release by creating a Brand Tribe because this allows members to address multiple goals which, in turn, boosts the dopamine release they experience. Importantly, sharing (whether active or passive) will strengthen the feeling of belonging to a Tribe, which will then trigger a dopamine hit whenever their 'Tribe' memory is activated. Thus you can expect members of a Brand Tribe to benefit from stronger and more frequent dopamine hits, which will ultimately benefit your brand.

8.5 How extreme should your disruption be?

Obviously, disruption requires innovation. You can't disrupt a market or competitive setting by simply doing what is already being done. You need new, innovative ways of competing. However, if your innovative new way of competing is too extreme, too far away what consumers consider acceptable, you will fail.

While many consumers like innovative new concepts and offers, remember that they are also attracted to the familiar. For a start, familiarity offers processing fluency – that is, it eliminates the need for extensive cognitive processing, thus saving energy. Secondly, familiarity typically leads to predictability and thus reduces or even eliminates (perceived) risk. Familiarity can also lead to habitualization, i.e., by repeating familiar processes like taking a particular product off the shelf when buying groceries, consumers habitualize the purchasing process and thus eliminate the need for any thinking at all.

Novelty, on the other hand, attracts attention. Especially when marketers want to change the way brands are perceived, they benefit from attracting attention. Most importantly, when brands mature it is necessary to disrupt the current mindset to get consumers to again see the brand as offering a great way to address one of their goals. This means that despite the benefits familiarity offers, there are marketing challenges that can only be addressed through novelty.

With both familiarity and novelty it is important not to take things too far. As the following chart shows, novelty that is overwhelming and familiarity that is boring will both lead to avoidance.

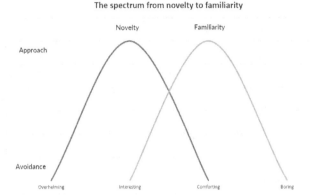

Illustration 13: *Source: Steve Genco, Andrew Pohlmann, Peter Steidl: Neuromarketing for Dummies, Wiley 2013*

It follows that your challenge is to offer sufficient novelty to attract attention, but not to an extent where consumers are rejecting the totally unfamiliar. As you will see several of the concepts I cover deal with this challenge by associating the disruptive brand positioning or offer with existing memories that have not previously been connected with the brand or offer.

9 Disrupting categorizations

As you know the nonconscious mind is always seeking shortcuts and a widely used shortcut is to categorize, eliminating the need to review each offer, brand or organization by simply lumping them together. For example, a consumer may think of banks or supermarkets as boring or unresponsive. This categorization shapes their relationships with these organizations: they don't want to invest time, money and effort, but rather minimize their contact with any of the organizations in the category they have established in their mind.

This creates a formidable marketing challenge when your brand is classified into a category the consumer rejects or feels indifferent to. In this section I explore categorizations and the strategies you can apply if your brand suffers from negative categorization.

How consumers categorize
The human mind uses the key elements of a brand or organization to determine which category it belongs to. Clearly, many brands belong to more than one category. As a simple example, think about a traditional supermarket, an online store like amazon (although the boundaries are getting blurred with amazon having launched into the bricks & mortar space) and a discount grocery chain. All are categorized as grocery stores, but they are also categorized into online or off-line, price categories, range offered, and so forth. The big question is 'What are the dominant criteria that frame the brand perception in the consumer's mind?'.

To make matters more complicated, the dominant criteria can change depending on the consumer's experience or goals the consumer wants to address. For example, a discount grocery store may be classified as offering good deals, but also fall into the categories 'boring to shop' and 'limited range'.

Brands can have a determining impact on how offers are

perceived. For example, at a time when Samsung outperformed the iPhone with respect to advanced features we have seen many Apple enthusiasts sticking with the iPhone because sporting the Apple brand was more important than product features. Said differently, the product may no longer have been placed into the *'leading technology'* category but the brand was in the *'most innovative'* category and thus overcame any deficiencies at the product level.

You are already familiar with the RTT which will allow you to check which category(ies) your brand is seen to fit into by consumers or specific consumer segments. An important question is what you can do if your brand has been categorized negatively, i.e., lumped together with other brands that are seen to have unfavorable qualities or capabilities. Let me illustrate this challenge by exploring a broad categorization that is typically made by the vast majority of consumers: the categorization into *Spend* versus *Save*.

The Spend and Save categories

We all tend to drift almost automatically towards anything that delivers emotional rewards. If you have a look at how you spend your time, you will most likely find that you have made more time to do what you like, and less time to do what you don't enjoy.

The result of your classifications is that your mind will try to allocate more resources – time, effort, money – to anything it has classified as a positive experience. By contrast, everything in the negative category will be drained of resources, so that the time, effort and money spent on these experiences will be minimized.

Once a product, service or brand has been placed into the Save category in the consumer's mind, the consumer will not be very responsive to any promotion that suggests a great experience can be had there. However, the consumer *is* likely to be receptive to an offer that allows them to spend less time, effort and/or money, as this is of course consistent with the Save strategy.

At the same time, the consumer will be keen to invest more time, effort and/or money into anything they have placed into the Spend category. For example, today's consumer is quite happy to spend a few dollars on a coffee or fresh juice as a treat while also being attracted to a supermarket special saving them two dollars. Many consumers are quite happy to wait for their drink for ten minutes at a juice bar but will be outraged when forced to spend the same length of time in a supermarket checkout or bank branch queue.

In retailing, this polarization has been a reality for a long time: we talk about '*doing the shopping*' when we refer to a shopping trip in the Save category, but '*going shopping*' when we refer to a pleasurable shopping trip we have placed into the Spend category because we enjoy it.

Doing the shopping is rational and explicit. Consumers often use a shopping list to get what they need. They consider their requirements but often resort to habitual buying when making their purchases because doing the shopping typically includes a large percentage of routine repeat purchases. G*oing shopping*, on the other hand, is emotional, exciting, exploratory. The whole idea is to be surprised, to enjoy the stimulation and to explore rather than just get the required items as quickly as possible. Clearly the purchase decisions are driven by goals, but these goals are often implicit and the consumer may be open to exploring different ways of addressing them.

Clearly, the more a consumer can save on *doing the shopping*, the more they can spend on *going shopping*. But the equation is much broader than this: the trade-off may lie in the purchase of an indulgence food or body care item, or time to sit down and enjoy a nice cup of coffee – all 'financed' by the savings in time, money and energy the consumer achieved when dealing with the necessary *doing the shopping* tasks.

Changing the code
Once a supermarket is seen to offer no sensory experience

worth having (no fun, excitement, involvement, feeling of success or deep satisfaction) and has been placed into the 'save' category, the supermarket's sole role in the consumer's life is as a place to save money, time and energy, thereby allowing the consumer to invest these resources into more rewarding activities. The code in the consumer's mind will filter out any messages that do not relate to savings, while letting messages that are on-code through to be processed by the consumer's brain. To change this code, you need to change the shopping experience.

Here is an example of how this can be done, at least with some shoppers: some time ago, Germany's trading house Tschibo developed a small display unit that can be placed into supermarkets and other stores. Every Monday it is stocked with a new range of goods offered at amazing prices not normally seen. So far this may sound just like a discount operation, but it is much more. First, the type of goods that will be offered each week is kept a secret. They could be anything – swimwear, kitchenware, electronic equipment, holiday travel deals, car accessories, imported wines, anything at all. Second, supply is limited, and once stocks are exhausted the offer disappears.

This means you are introducing expectation, surprise and the excitement of hunting into the supermarket-shopping equation. Consumers don't know what that week's product theme will be, so they must hurry into their local supermarket if they want to make sure they can buy before stock has been exhausted. It is the exact opposite of conventional supermarket shopping, which is list-driven, predictable and unlikely to lead to surprises beyond the usual price discounts. Moving a brand from the save to the spend category is a major effort that requires creative thinking and a willingness to try something unconventional.

The alternative is to focus on how to help the consumer 'save.' The most common approach is the use of discounts and special offers. This is a means of making the trade-off more favorable so the consumer feels that investing their time, money and energy was worthwhile because they got one or more great deals. However, it is important to keep in mind that introducing ways of saving money by offering discounts, or of saving time and energy through, say, self-scanning at the checkout, will do little to engage consumers and get them to change their overall relationship with the supermarket. They will still want to get in and out as quickly as possible and are likely to maintain a very basic, functional relationship with the retailer.

The key question is this: Is your objective to add more value by giving the consumer a better trade-off on their time, money and energy investment? Or is your objective to develop a long-term, positive relationship with the consumer by disrupting the perception that shopping (of the 'doing the shopping' variety) is essentially a necessary evil, representing a function that is important but not liked?

10 Brand Vision Archetypes
Who do you want your brand to be known as?

We have built a sound foundation for the development of brand strategies. However, there is one important element still missing: How should you present your brand or, more specifically: 'WHO do you want your brand to be known as?'

As a simple illustration imagine you are briefing your advertising agency, stressing that the brand to be advertised is one that you want to invest in, and the key associations you want to develop with your brand are 'fun' and 'enjoyment'.

This is a terrible brief. It does not provide your agency with a clear understand of the qualities of the brand it is supposed to help build. Their communications program could focus on exploring something new or on being adventurous, it could present the brand as being the ultimate arbiter on how to enjoy life, or it could focus on exploring new and different ways to have fun. The brand could be presented as standing for progress or for stability, it could be extravert or introvert. And these are just some of the options.

What is missing from your brief is a clear understanding of *who* you want your brand to be known as. Remember I mentioned brand codes a few pages back. To develop a brand code you have to be consistent in the way the brand is presented at all key touchpoints. An important aspect of being consistent is the brand's personality, i.e., who the brand is.

The most effective – if not the *only* effective – way to get consistency across all key touchpoints is to identify a brand vision archetype and to ensure that this archetype is consistently brought alive at all touchpoints.

The brand vision archetype is not a concept that was discovered by neuroscience. Its foundation is empirical rather than scientific in nature. Yet this concept offers a holistic approach to positioning a brand that is consistent with the proposition that a brand is a memory, and that it is the marketer's responsibility to shape this memory in a way that creates an internally consistent, holistic and meaningful brand perception.

From brand pyramids to brand vision archetypes[17]
Traditionally, the vision for a brand was derived and presented in a rational, analytical way. Attributes that were supposed to characterize the brand and define what it stands for were used to communicate the brand to those who needed to understand it: the planners who defined the brand strategy, the marketing executives who made the decisions, and the creative people in the advertising agency who (hopefully!) translated these dry descriptions into emotionally powerful communication. Even the consumer was supposed to understand these analytical descriptions, with much market research based on rating brands against these attributes and with communications that quite often attempted to directly portray a particular quality deemed to be key to the brand's positioning.

There are three problems with this approach:
- First, it diminishes differentiation. Too many brands are seeking to portray and stand for the same abstract qualities, such as being innovative, consumer friendly, welcoming, grounded, trustworthy, able to make life easy, exciting, and so forth.
- Second, much gets lost in the translation: attributes such as 'welcoming,' 'grounded' or 'exciting' mean different things to different people – and even to the same person at different times, depending on the context and prevailing mood.
- Third, the human mind thinks holistically. We

---

[17] The sections on brand vision archetypes and touchpoints have been adapted from Kim Boehm & Peter Steidl, *Brand Vision Archetypes: Creating Brands With Meaning*, NMSBA 2016. This book presents step-by-step guidelines for using brand vision archetypes and includes a set of brand-vision-archetype cards with detailed descriptions for each archetype for immediate use.

experience a brand in its totality (if at all), not as a set of abstract attributes.

Fortunately, this problem can be resolved through the use of archetypes. Because we all intuitively recognize the same archetypes, they form a universal language that is neither segment- nor culture-specific. Importantly, archetypes not only embody certain qualities but we also seem to understand them in a holistic, intuitive way. In other words, we '*know*' how a particular archetype would behave in a certain situation, what an archetype would think about an issue, or what values an archetype represents. This makes archetypes an extremely powerful tool when developing a brand vision.

Archetypes are being used effectively by some of the world's leading corporations and their advertising agencies. However, beyond this small, elite group, their use is sporadic and often not well understood, often leading to some questionable applications.

Let's start with an example: Adidas versus Nike. You would most likely come up with the same list of attributes for both companies: dynamic, young, aggressive, stylish, delivering advanced technologies, edgy, et cetera. You might well conclude that there is a lack of brand differentiation. However, by using brand vision archetypes, you can immediately see how these brands could be differentiated. (I say 'could be' as neither Nike nor Adidas adhere strictly to their stated positioning.)

Nike encourages you to give it a try and to see how far you can go. Its tag line '*Just Do It!*' encourages you to explore your limits rather than stay in your comfort zone. Nike is an *Explorer* brand. Adidas, on the other hand, is a *Warrior* brand. Its call to action is '*Impossible is Nothing.*' If you don't believe this – if you just want to test your limits rather than be convinced that you will conquer – then don't buy Adidas, buy Nike!

I personally have no doubt that a holistic rather than analytical approach would serve the strategic as well as the creative process much better, but is there any evidence to support such an assertion? Indeed there is.

The well-known psychologist Carl Jung believed that there is a core of knowledge that all humans have from birth. He coined the phrase *'collective unconscious'* to refer to this shared, intuitive knowledge we pass on from generation to generation. Empirical research suggests that this might well be the case. In the 1970s and 1980s, Joseph Campbell documented the universality of mythic forms and characters. He collected stories from every corner of the globe – primitive, modern, ancient and contemporary.[18] Campbell discovered that while their names differ, a small number of characters recur and are found everywhere. Campbell also demonstrated that there are only a limited number of mythic forms and that these, too, are universal.

It is worth mentioning that Joseph Campbell became an advisor to a number of Hollywood studios. For example, the movie *'Star Wars'* benefited from Campbell's guidance on archetype development. Each character represents a particular archetype, which is why *'Star Wars'* is such a compelling story. In the advertising arena, Dr. Joseph Plummer used brand vision archetypes extensively over many decades. In fact, many enduring brand icons, such as the Marlboro Man and the Jolly Green Giant, are reportedly based on archetypes.

From our point of view, it doesn't really matter whether we are born with this knowledge or whether we are destined to pick it up during the early years of our lives. The point is that we all *'know'* the same archetypes and thus can communicate with others at a level that transcends language. (It is important to keep in mind that archetypes are not stereotypes. Stereotypes are transient – they represent a type of person that may be

---

[18] Joseph Campbell, *The Hero with a Thousand Faces*, 2nd edition, New World Library, 2008; Joseph Campbell and Bill Moyers, *The Power of Myth*, Anchor, 1991; Joseph Campbell, *Myths to Live By*, Penguin, 1993.

typical in a particular context and time – whereas archetypes are permanently engrained in our thinking, across time and cultures.)

Importantly, when a brand consistently brings an archetype alive, it is more likely that the consumer will develop a code for this brand, i.e., a very clear idea as to how, when and where the brand can contribute to addressing a goal. A strong brand code will differentiate your brand and boost its market share. Brand vision archetypes are a means of making this happen.

The choice of a brand vision archetype depends on:
- the brand's qualities and capabilities, i.e., what it can realistically deliver
- its perceived strengths and weaknesses, i.e., its credibility
- the long-term objectives, i.e., the aspirations of the company
- the target market's receptiveness
- the competitive landscape, i.e., which archetypes are already embodied by competitive brands.

How many brand archetypes do you need?

For some strange reason advocates of an archetype practice seem to like the idea of presenting 12 brand archetypes. However, they each tend to select a somewhat different set to make up their 12. After becoming thoroughly confused by looking at the various archetype collections, my collaborator Kim Boehm and I went back to the work of Jung and Campbell and, pragmatically allowing our own consulting practice to influence the final selection, we were able to identify some 28 different archetypes.[19]

One of the problems when working with a more narrow set of archetypes, such as an arbitrarily selected dozen, is that the resulting brand visions will lack the desired degree of specificity, which in turn will diminish

---

[19] see Kim Boehn & Peter Steidl, *Creating Brands With Meaning*, NMSBA 2016.

differentiation opportunities in the market place. To illustrate this point, let's take the Explorer and the Adventurer archetypes. At a superficial level, both seem to 'do' the same thing; i.e., they engage in exciting activities, move actively through life, and seek experiences. However, their motivation is very different:

The Adventurer is a *thrill seeker*. The thrill, rather than the activity itself, is what motivates the Adventurer. Naturally, new activities are an important part of the mix because new experiences are more likely to offer a thrill, but the Adventurer will also repeat experiences that consistently provide a thrill.

Explorers use new experiences to *reflect and learn more* – often about themselves. They are on a journey they hope will take them closer to understanding. The thrills are secondary; the reflection is primary.

When you consider this, you realize that the Adventurer and Explorer are very different indeed, even though they may both engage in a variety of new activities and seek similar experiences: the Adventurer seeks to be thrilled, the Explorer to learn more.

Clearly the archetype determines how the brand will behave and what it offers the consumer, because it encapsulates a distinct motivation for that behavior. It therefore follows that quite often we have to delve a bit deeper than overt behavior to understand archetypes. Another example is the Guardian and the Master:

The Guardian is a perfectionist who will try to improve any processes, systems or rules whenever they may help to *protect* whatever it is the Guardian is charged with protecting.

The Master is also a perfectionist. However, Masters seek perfection *for themselves*. They want to be perfect with respect to a particular skill or capability they have decided to focus on.

Again, the Master and the Guardian may display some similar behavioral traits, but their underlying motivation is very different and thus the choices they make will often be quite different too. For the Master perfectionism is an end in itself, while for the Guardian perfectionism is a means, with protection being the end.

Masterbrands, for example, are typically Guardians – they provide some credibility and familiarity, but most importantly they protect the buyer by guaranteeing the quality of the product brand they buy. So when you buy Dove or Lipton Tea, the Unilever masterbrand guarantees that the product you buy will be up to Unilever's standards. The masterbrand endorsement reduces risk. But masterbrands are rarely Masters.

Who the brand wants to be known as

Here is the important point: the issue is not *what* a brand could do or might do, the question is *who* you want the brand to be known as. By selecting a particular archetype and living this archetype, the brand will be understood as that archetype. There will be clarity, and consumers will be able to develop a meaningful relationship with the brand because they know *who* it is.

Clearly, many brands do not represent archetypes. They have fuzzy images because they have not 'lived' a particular archetype. They have a confused personality, and their values and actions are not well understood. In other words, they have failed to develop a brand code.

By using brand vision archetypes, you can introduce some meaning into the equation. Consumers can then start to understand the brand, as you have provided the basis for a relationship to develop. By choosing the right brand vision archetype you not only introduce meaning but also make the brand relevant to its target group. Your target group can relate to the brand and understand which goals your brand can contribute to realizing. In other words, you are developing and shaping a brand code in the consumer's mind.

Finally, I need to stress that the choice of a brand vision archetype is one that the custodians of the brand have to make. Market research can tell you whether consumers believe a brand represents a particular archetype, but consumers can't identify the most appropriate brand vision archetype to move forward with. The challenge is for the marketer to find an archetype that embodies the brand vision.

When should you change your brand vision archetype?
Positioning a brand is a long-term, strategic decision. By consistently bringing your brand vision archetype alive, you are creating a brand code in the minds of your target consumers. Frequent changes in positioning are likely to confuse the market and make it impossible to establish a brand code.

However, the brand positioning needs to be reviewed when there are significant, long-term changes in the market (i.e., in the goals consumers have) or in the competitive landscape (i.e., how consumers believe these goals can be satisfied). You also need to review your brand positioning should the brand mature or decline (i.e., your brand code starts to lack relevance or grows weaker through rare activation). However, often it is not necessary to change the brand vision archetype when your challenge is to revitalize a brand. Rather, it is simply a matter of bringing the brand vision archetype alive in innovative new ways that refresh your brand code. The actual archetype should only be changed if you need to consider a massive, strategic change in brand positioning.

Finally, I need to stress that the brand vision archetype should not only determine the design of the brand's touchpoints in the market place, but also its touchpoints with employees, suppliers, investors, intermediaries and any other important target groups. The brand needs to be consistent across all key target groups, but the specific messages and touchpoints will naturally vary by audience. These variations simply present relevant ways of bringing the brand vision archetype alive with the different groups.

Touchpoint engineering: Bringing brand vision archetypes alive

Touchpoint engineering is the critical core issue when you adopt a brand vision archetype. Choosing a brand vision archetype – which is typically done in a workshop environment – is the easy part. Finding effective ways of bringing this archetype alive is the challenge, and this must be addressed effectively.

The reason should be obvious: the brand strategy and associated brand vision archetypes 'live' only in the marketer's mind and in the strategy documents they may have developed. All the consumer is exposed to are the signals sent at key touchpoints. Thus, the impact of the strategy depends on these signals, not on the intent embodied in the marketer's mind or in the prepared blueprints. If you can't bring your preferred brand vision archetype alive, then the choice is unacceptable and a different archetype needs to be chosen. This is why I spend far more time in brand vision archetype workshops exploring how preferred archetypes could be brought alive, than on the initial choice of the archetype.

Essentially, the task is to review the key touchpoints where the consumer 'meets' the brand and ensure they are all aligned and that they bring the chosen brand vision archetypes (primary and secondary) alive. The key decisions to be made focus on which touchpoints should be:

- *adapted* to ensure they bring the brand vision archetypes alive as intended
- *created* to broaden or intensify the experience the target group has with the brand
- *left as they are* because they already deliver the right experience, or
- *deleted* because they are not creating the right experience and/or are irrelevant.

Obviously, it is also important to document *why* certain touchpoints need to be changed, deleted, kept the same or created and *how* this should be achieved. A timetable will help to guide implementation.

As I said earlier, it is crucial to bear in mind that a brand vision archetype that cannot be brought alive in a meaningful and high impact way is not an appropriate choice. While you may feel the archetype in question would be right for the brand, there is no point in adopting it if you can't create exposures that convince your target groups that this is truly *who* your brand is. You would merely end up in a fantasy world where wishful thinking leads, in the end, to frustration and failure.

It follows that you need to review your brand vision archetype selection if your touchpoint analysis and associated engineering strategies suggest that you won't succeed. If you can't find ways of bringing your preferred brand vision archetype(s) alive, then you must go back to the drawing board and select another one.

11 Strategic segmentation
Meaningful segmentation on the basis of purchase drivers

What is the purpose of segmentation? The underlying concept is that, by aligning your strategy more closely with the purchase drivers of the group of consumers you are targeting, you will be more effective in influencing their purchase decisions.

There are two important points here: First, if you want to base your brand strategies on your segmentation it is imperative that you segment on the basis of purchase drivers. Second, if you segment the market the same way your competitor does, you will end up taking more or less the same approach to aligning your strategy more closely with these purchase drivers. This is why in many markets there is in fact little difference in the overall strategies competitors pursue. There are differences in creative ideas and their executions, but the overall strategies are often very similar.

Ideally, you should use segmentation to find a new and different way to slice up the market that will benefit your brands. You are seeking to define segments differently to the way your competitors define their segments by focusing on an advantage your brand has, such as being able to address a particular goal more effectively than other brands. Such segmentation provides fertile ground for developing an innovative, highly differentiated, and possibly disruptive brand strategy because you can see segments that eluded your competitors or that they simply can't target effectively.

Earlier in my career I was heavily involved in segmentation studies which were exploratory in nature. The idea was to use multivariate analyzes to create a range of different segmentations and to explore for each segmentation option to what degree it would facilitate the development of highly differentiated brand strategies. When used like that, segmentation is a strategic tool. When you simply put brands on a pre-determined map, defined for everybody by the same dimensions, you are missing the key benefit segmentation offers: to explore different strategic options that would benefit your brand specifically.

It is a great pity that many research agencies are selling standard segmentation approaches and, ironically, often on the basis that many leading firms are using these approaches. Of course this is much more profitable than exploring unique segmentation options for each client but, quite frankly, if somebody told me that my competitors are using these segmentation approaches I would immediately reject them. I don't want to be a follower who accepts or even takes comfort from conventions. Effective marketing is not just about doing the same things better than competitors, but doing things differently.

Another problem you are likely to encounter is an inadequate methodology. Many segmentation studies are based on consumers' stated attitudes, preferences, opinions and intentions. As you know, these are less than reliable as such rationalizations are not what drives brand choice.

Then you will find needs segmentations pretending to be goal segmentations. As I have already said, 'goals' and what are commonly termed 'needs' are not the same: needs are rationalizations while most goals are nonconscious in nature and cannot be detected by direct questioning. Some research agencies claim to take a neuroscience-based approach, for example by using a set of different faces or emojis to let the consumer choose how they feel about a particular attribute or desire. They do not seem to understand that giving a person a set of answers to choose from – whether these be images or words – engages the rational, analytical mind. You might ask yourself *'Is it more like face/emoji no.3 or 4?'* and at this stage you are fully into analytical thinking mode. This is why the Response Time Test I discussed earlier only allows for a 'yes', 'no' or 'can't say' answer.

When it comes to goals, consumers are likely to share (most of) the same basic physiological goals, but are likely to have differentiated emotional goals. Marketers naturally want to identify the high potential goal segments they should target. Goal segmentation represents a major advance on traditional segmentation practices:

- First, you are not limiting yourself to a particular demographic, socioeconomic or psychographic segment – goals are often shared across many, sometimes all, of these segments.

  For example, young and old, wealthy and poor, educated and uneducated, males and females may all share the goal to be excited, to belong, to connect, to dominate, and so on. Naturally, there is often a particular demographic, socioeconomic or psychographic segment that contains somewhat more consumers than other segments that share a particular goal, but you should not limit your focus to this segment. Whenever possible, you should focus on how your brand can satisfy a goal across all those consumers who share this goal.

- Second, you are not focusing your marketing efforts on the personal characteristics of consumers but on what actually drives their purchase decision, i.e., the goals you want them to believe your brand can address more effectively than competing options.

- Third, you are identifying the key emotions through your segmentation, allowing you to then capture these emotions in all of the important exposures consumers have to your brand.

The problem does not lie in identifying goals that may drive purchase decisions and thus should be included in your segmentation study. The German/UK neuro-marketing consulting firm Decode, for example, uses the following segmentation approach:

- *Adventure*: freedom, courage, rebellion, discovery, risk
- *Autonomy*: pride, success, power, superiority, recognition

- *Discipline*: precision, order, logic, reason
- *Security*: care, trust, closeness, security, warmth
- *Enjoyment*: relaxation, light heartedness, openness, pleasure
- *Excitement*: vitality, fun, curiosity, creativity, change

Meanwhile a German consulting group developed the Limbic Segmentation concept that has been licensed to a number of firms around the world, focusing on:
- Adventure, Thrill
- *Dominance*
- Discipline, Control
- *Balance*
- Indulgence, Imagination
- *Stimulation*

These and other segmentation approaches share the same underlying objective: to capture the key drivers of the consumer's purchase decision. However, there remains a major problem: the data is based on asking consumers questions they cannot answer correctly as they do not have access to their nonconscious mind. The obvious solution is to use the Response Time Test you are already familiar with.

First, you can use the Response Time Test to get a reliable reading on the relative importance of attributes, capabilities and qualities. This will allow you to identify segments that are seeking the qualities your brand offers. But you can do even better than that: you can also assess which attributes, capabilities and qualities are 'owned' by certain brands in the consumer's minds, which are shared between brands and which are not (yet) owned by anyone. This provides a much more meaningful market segmentation as it is aligned with what drives purchase decisions.

The other option – only open to you if you have a data lake with extensive behavioral data – is to infer the key drivers of behavior by looking at what consumers actually do, i.e., the choices they actually make, what they buy, how they spend their leisure time, what they invest in, et cetera.

Consumers with specific goals typically find a variety of different ways to satisfy their goals, and this means that their goals are reflected in their behavior. For example, a consumer with a strong excitement/adventure goal may:
- take adventure holidays
- buy a car that is positioned on an adventure platform
- try different foods
- read magazines and books that tell adventure stories
- see adventure movies and television shows
- engage in adventurous leisure time activities (like abseiling, rock climbing, hang gliding, etc.)
- follow celebrities who often play adventure type roles
- and so on.

Because of limited time, money, availability and ability they will typically not satisfy their goal in all theoretically possible ways, but their behavior is likely to nevertheless show a number of indicators that allow us to classify them as 'Adventurers'.

Let's assume you have identified consumers who seek adventure or who like to expose themselves to adventure through movies, television, You Tube downloads, and so on. The next step is to find out if these adventurers are satisfying their goal by:
- buying your brand
- buying in the category but not your brand
- not buying in the category.

You can determine your communications challenge on the basis of this assessment:
- **Buying your brand** – these consumers already see your brand as addressing their 'adventure' goal. You simply have to reinforce their belief that your brand offers an effective way to address their goal.
- **Buying in the category but not your brand** – these consumers use the type of product your brand offers to satisfy their 'adventure' goal, but see other brands in the category as satisfying this goal more effectively than does your brand. The challenge is to convince them that your brand offers a very effective way of addressing their goal. Your competitors are *brands in*

the same category.
- **Not buying in the category** – while these consumers have an 'adventure' goal they address this goal with products from *other* categories. Your challenge is to convince them that your brand can satisfy their goal effectively. Your competitors are *brands in different categories*.

While the goal segmentation gives you a clear focus and a meaningful platform for developing your communications and creative strategy, it needs to be calibrated by taking into account barriers to purchase. These barriers may include affordability, usability, and bad experiences with past purchases.

I also need to add that a behavioral approach as outlined above works quite well with goals that tend to manifest themselves in specific actions and decisions. The same approach may struggle to identify sufficient evidence when dealing with goals that are less likely to result in actions that can be observed, or when actions are difficult to interpret. Nevertheless you can always learn a lot about the market by exploring what consumers actually do, typically resulting in greater insights than a traditional segmentation approach using a set of demographic, socioeconomic and psychographic variables that have no clear link to the drivers of a purchase. I have used this approach with a leading global communications firm and we were able to identify segments defined by dopamine (generated by different kinds of behavior). This provided us with a very different view of the market, allowing for the development of innovative, even disruptive, brand strategies.

Finally, you can simply align your offer with Deep Rooted Drivers of Behavior (DRDs). We know that these DRDs result in goals. You don't have to do any research – this is a biological certainty. You can position your brand as offering the most effective way of addressing these goals.

Strategic and executional segmentation

Before moving on I should articulate the difference between strategy level and execution level segmentation. Strategic segmentation – as the name suggests – should define the brand's positioning, core offer and key messages. When it comes to execution there tend to be a variety of distinct communications channels (and sometimes also distribution channels) that allow the marketer to adapt how the core offer is presented to specific sub-segments. It follows that detail is important when it comes to execution, but should be avoided when focusing on strategy.

There are also typically differences in focus. Strategic segmentation should be based on purchase drivers and, as goals drive purchase decisions, you should pursue a goal segmentation.

When it comes to *execution* you may want to reach a number of sub-segments given today's variety of communications channels, and an understanding of how these segments address the same goal differently will be important. But the strategic brand positioning, core offer and message should remain the same.

Major pitfalls many segmentation studies share include:
- Over-segmenting the market, resulting in a multitude of segments that are far too small to warrant a significant marketing investment. The argument typically put forward is *'Well, this small segment is the sweet spot but we will obviously cover other segments as well, so we do get to target a sizeable chunk of the market!'* This is, of course, total nonsense. Why rely on a spill-over effect rather than segment the market in a meaningful way?
- Applying the same segmentation approach used by competitors, which delivers the same perspective competitors have, rather than defining segments differently to create a platform for strategic differentiation.
- Using segmentation variables that are not actual purchase drivers, such as stated needs, attitudes,

opinions or beliefs.
- Looking only for differences between segments rather than also for similarities that would allow you to focus on much larger segments in an effective and meaningful way.
- Segmenting the same way at both the strategy and execution levels.

The emergence of new segments
A segmentation study delivers a snapshot of the market as it is today. This is obviously useful and important as your strategies have to be effective in today's market. However, it is also important to be aware of – and to monitor – changes evolving over a longer period of time that are likely to have a material impact on your target group's receptiveness to your messages in general and your brand in particular.

One of these long-term changes is the way the digital environment changes the responsiveness, focus and even values of consumers.

Much has been written and said about 'digital natives', those people who have grown up fully immersed in the digital world. These young people have not known a world without internet or mobile phone; they are used to GPS and Google Maps when it comes to finding their way; they search the internet for immediate answers to any of their questions; they connect more often online than face-to-face; they shop and transact more often online than in the real world; they use Apps to tell them when to sleep, eat or exercise; and we could undoubtedly add many more differences between this generation and their parents'.

On one hand, the digital environment plays into the hands of the young as they are best able to work out how to make use of it. They tend to have more experience than many older people with gadgets and software, so they have better intuitive insight into how such things work. There is also no doubt that social media in particular delivers the recognition and rewards many people crave.

On the other hand, the digital environment supports superficiality. Social media is an obvious example. The vast majority of Facebook and Twitter posts are about things that are so unimportant and anecdotal that you would almost certainly not have talked about them had you met your so-called 'friends' face-to-face. Rather than encouraging you to learn about complexity, causality and relevance social media emphasizes superficiality.

It would be reasonable to expect that digital immersion will have an impact on how the brain develops. It therefore won't come as a surprise that an immersive digital environment impacts on how we think, feel and act.

As you know, the brain will adapt to whatever demands we make on it[20] After all, brain plasticity suggests that anything we do a lot of will be accommodated by the brain, which will rearrange neurons and connections to align resources with where we apparently need them. In other words it is not so much the brain that determines what we are good at, but our own actions, with the brain a willing supporter of whatever it is that we do a lot of. We can therefore safely assume that frequent immersion in digital environments will have an impact on how we feel, think and act.

Not surprisingly, there are two schools of thought about what this means: some experts claim that the digital environment makes us smarter, while others show evidence that it has a negative impact. The reason for this divergence of opinion lies largely in what different experts feel is important.

There is no doubt that the digital environment does have a positive impact on the efficiency of your hardware. It trains your brain to deal with fast moving exposures, multiple inputs, and parallel tasks. (Note that you can't actually 'multitask' in that you can't in fact do two things that require conscious processing at once, but the brain

---

[20] See Peter Steidl, *Smarter, Wiser, Calmer, Focused: Your brain's natural advantage*, Createspace 2016

can get very good at jumping quickly between tasks without you even realizing it.) Manufacturers and interface designers are also trying to allow for an intuitive approach to using equipment and software. This means that people who run their lives essentially online are likely to develop a strong intuitive sense of how to progress and find what they want.

These are some positive developments because an immersion in the digital world allows these consumers to:
- boost their ability to work out how to use technology and software - which is, after all, a very important ability these days
- reduce their reaction time
- get better at 'multi-tasking', i.e., getting their brain used to switching quickly from one task to another
- engage in a wider scope of activities – these are likely to be superficial, but nevertheless they are exposed to many different contexts.

However, there are also some downsides:
- Spending time on social media rather than face-to-face with other people leads to under-developed social skills. The very important nuances – facial expression, tone of voice, body movements, et cetera – are either not transmitted or are not as apparent when we interact online. Even in a video conference or call we don't receive the finer nuances of behavior that express how the other person reacts or feels.
- As online answers are available to most questions, digital natives spend much less time exploring contexts and options. They are less likely to discuss the problems they are seeking solutions for with others as they can often find some sort of answer online, making further discussions unnecessary. This lack of exploration means that solutions may be found quickly, but they may well not be very good solutions. But the more significant issue is the resulting lack of exploration skills, as it means that they tend to be less well-equipped when it comes to dealing with complex problems than people who have trained their mind to explore contexts and relationships.

- The internet's ability to let us choose exactly what we want leads many people to associate with and get information solely from third parties who hold the same views as they do. If we dislike something we are likely to read the blogs or reports or watch the videos or 'talk' to people who share this dislike with us. And if we like something the same happens. This means that our views are constantly reinforced, strengthening our beliefs and, in the process, possibly turning us into single-minded people.
- The time spent online is not additional time we suddenly have at your disposal. Rather, it is time we would have spent pursuing other activities and interests. We might have been more physically active, had more regular and better quality meals, met and talked with more people face-to-face, entertained more often, and so on. The variety and depth of real life boosts the brain's capacity and slows down its decline.
- We decrease our enjoyment of life. Research has shown that people who take pictures of their food in a restaurant or during a concert (or on a multitude of other occasions) experience less involvement, excitement and satisfaction than those who just focus on what they are doing or are part of at the time. The same applies to using a tablet or smartphone while watching television. It's okay when the program is boring and we don't want to listen, but if it is an enjoyable program we get less enjoyment out of it if we interrupt our viewing by doing something else, even if it is related to the program.
- We limit our creativity. We may in fact do things you might not have done otherwise, such as photo shop pictures we have taken, but whenever we use an app we are essentially limiting our creativity to whatever the app allows us to do. We don't explore and create the way we do off-line.
- We do not train our ability to orient ourselves, and dumb down our natural ability to do so, by relying on GPS for navigation.
- We limit the opportunity to learn how to create

compelling, well-structured arguments. The shorthand typical for online exchanges encourages a superficial and rather primitive communication style.

As time passes the segment of consumers who have spent most or all of their live immersed in the digital environment is obviously going to grow, thus making it important for any marketer to understand how this emerging segment thinks and behaves differently. One of many important aspects is that an immersion in the digital world is likely to accelerate the adoption of a digital persona/home assistant which, as I explain elsewhere, will have a significant impact on purchasing behavior.

Part III
Execution

The word 'strategy' may be one of the most over-used terms in marketing today. Everybody seems to be working to a 'strategy' – communications agencies, consultants and their clients all talk about their digital strategy, social media strategy, innovation strategy, and so on. However, most of these 'strategies' are actually executions of a higher level strategy. A social media strategy is an element of the execution of a digital strategy. A digital strategy is an element of the execution of a communications strategy. A communications strategy is an element of the execution of a brand strategy. A brand strategy is an element of the execution of a marketing strategy, which in turn is an element of the execution of a business strategy.

Let me assure you that this is not just about semantics. The problem is that in most instances the necessary links between these 'strategies' have not been established and thought through properly. This may, for example, lead to an isolated social media strategy that is not a great execution of the brand strategy. It may contain some novel ideas or execute a particular concept brilliantly, but this does not turn it into a strategy. Similarly, advertising strategies are far too often disconnected from a brand or marketing strategy.

The end result is a fragmented set of activities that will not deliver the impact you could have had. Furthermore, the lack of integration leads to giving agencies and consultants too much freedom, resulting in a greater workload for the client who is left trying to put the overall program together to reduce the fragmentation that has been caused by this inadequate approach.

In my experience the brand strategy needs to have a central role. Of course we need a marketing strategy that integrates across brands and aggregates the contributions to be done by the various teams responsible for sales, R&D, manufacturing, and so on. But if we have an integrated brand strategy that considers the portfolio of brands and brings together an integrated set of executions – the touchpoints we plan to utilize, the messages we plan to send at these touchpoints, the innovations we want to develop and leverage – then many of the elements will fall into place.

For this third and final section I will cover a selection of important aspects related to executing your strategy. If you expect a planning blueprint you will be disappointed. If you are looking for a refresh and coverage of important, but often neglected, aspects of execution you should find these final chapters useful.

12 Marketing communications

Important:
I need to clarify that here I am using 'ad' as shorthand for 'touchpoint'. The principles outlined in this chapter apply regardless of the type of exposure (passive, active or interactive) or the media used to deliver it (i.e., traditional broadcast or digital media, including social media).

I stated earlier that marketing communications should facilitate the execution of the brand strategy. In fact for many brands, and especially consumer brands, communications can be a hugely influential element of the marketing program.

Naturally, everything I have covered in Part 1 about the consumer's mind is relevant - and important - when it comes to developing a communications program. How you set your campaign objectives will be influenced by whether your brand is a habitual or a considered purchase, and whether your campaign will aim primarily at the nonconscious or the conscious mind. Similarly, your communications strategy and its execution will need to reflect any brand, product, category or other relevant code you have identified, and needs to ensure your adopted brand vision archetype(s) is(are) being brought alive at key touchpoints.

While I have covered these points in some detail already, I want to address some very important aspects that are specific to marketing communications.

First, you need to explore in much greater depth the question of which of the two consumer's minds - the conscious or the nonconscious mind - you should be aiming at. This has significant implications when it comes to your communications strategy, creative development and execution.

Second, you need to differentiate between the 'ad memory' you are creating with your marketing communications activities and the 'brand memory' you attempt to shape to impact on sales.

Third, there are a number of specific issues, such as the impact of ad-skipping and ad blocking, the importance of mood congruency, priming, digital media and measuring advertising effectiveness.

Several of these issues sit at the intersection of strategy, creative and media and may well provide more fuel for the seemingly endless argument in favor of or against a full-service agency. Before we look at these challenges in greater depth, let me summarize the key differences between a traditional approach to advertising and a neurobranding approach:

Traditional approach	**Neurobranding approach**
Get the consumer's attention	*Nonconscious processing can be more effective*
Consumers make rational decisions	*Purchases are driven by emotional, largely nonconscious goals*
Attitudes drive behavior	*Behavior often drives attitudes*
We need to present a compelling reason to buy	*We can shape the brand memory, leading to sales down the track*
We need a huge campaign burst	*We need sensory rich, diverse media to establish an ad memory that can be activated in a cost-efficient way*
We need to refresh by repeatedly using the ad	*We need continuous activation of the ad memory by triggering just an element of this memory*
We make media choices on the basis of proven effectiveness in reaching the target audience	*Different media have different natural advantages when it comes to creating a rich ad memory*
We need to make sure consumers recall the ad memory	*We need to make sure our ad is linked to the brand memory*
Ads have little or no impact when fast forwarded	*The ad memory is activated when the ad is fast forwarded as long as a full ad memory has previously been established*

Ads should be placed into media that make logical sense (e.g., a car ad in Top Gear)	*Ads should be placed in a media context that is emotionally congruent*
Engagement and activity measures (likes, downloads, clicks, etc.) tell us how effective our digital media ads or social media campaign have been	*Engagement and activity measures do not tell us anything about the effectiveness of our digital ads or social media initiatives*
Effectiveness can be measured by asking consumers to recall ads, to tell us if they had an impact on how they feel about a brand, or to report on likelihood of purchase.	*Consumers can't explicitly tell us anything about the impact of ads because ads are largely processed by their nonconscious mind and they don't know why they do what they do nor what they will do in the future.*

The following pages explore the key elements of a neurobranding based communications approach in greater depth.

Are you targeting the conscious or the nonconscious mind?

It is important to remember that the nonconscious mind drives most purchases. It even has a significant impact on the purchase decision when consumers deliberate and analyze with their conscious mind, because nonconscious judgment heuristics are likely to shape these deliberations and the resulting purchase decisions.

So forget the AIDA formula - Attention, Interest, Desire, Action – if you have grown up with it. Not that long ago, the prevalent view was that an ad has to present a compelling argument in favor of the brand or product (i.e., aim at the conscious mind). This implied that the consumer has to give the message attention and that some cognitive processing has to take place for the ad to have an impact. Challenges like breaking through the boredom barrier were primary considerations because an ad that did not generate attention was considered to have failed.

However, neuroscience has demonstrated that it is

the nonconscious mind that largely determines how the consumer feels and thinks about brands and products, and this is what ultimately drives the purchase decision. As the nonconscious cannot engage in cognitive processing it is guided by signals and contexts more than by specific messages.

Let's look again at the two alternative paths that can lead to a purchase decision. While both approaches ultimately aim at generating sales, the paths chosen to reach that end are quite different.

Advertising aiming at the *nonconscious mind* focuses on:
- building emotional connections
- encouraging nonconscious processing by avoiding a rational argument that engages the conscious mind
- priming/activating judgment heuristics
- shaping the brand memory in a way that favors the brand when it comes to addressing certain goals.

While with advertising aiming at the *conscious mind* the focus is on:
- getting the consumer's attention
- presenting a compelling argument
- engaging the conscious mind, i.e., getting the consumer to think about the offer or particular features or qualities the brand offers.

Data drawn from the IPA Effectiveness Awards in the UK, comprising of 1,400 case studies gathered over three decades, shows that emotional content tends to be more effective than exclusively rational content. 31 percent of ads with exclusively emotional content resulted in large profit gains, compared with only 16 percent of ads with exclusively rational content. Mixed emotional and rational content ads ended up somewhere in the middle with 26 percent.

While emotions are not responsible for making the sale (this is the realm of addressing goals, which in turn triggers emotions), these statistics are

compelling. But it is important to choose the right approach for the specific marketing challenge at hand rather than simply doing what works more often. From a neuroscience perspective aiming at the nonconscious mind works because:
- consumers typically do not go through a rational assessment of options when facing a purchase decision
- in fact many purchases are habitual in nature, with no engagement by the conscious mind
- purchase decisions are likely to be influenced by judgment heuristics
- the nonconscious mind is likely to assign value and meaning to the offer and how it is presented (including ads, pricing, packaging, et cetera) well before the slower conscious mind kicks in with any rational consideration.

This does not mean that aiming at the conscious mind is never an effective option. The all-important decision you will have to make is:
- Are you trying to get the consumer's attention, present a compelling argument, and convince them that buying your brand is the best option (aiming at the consumer's conscious mind)?
- Or are you trying to influence the consumer's purchase decision through priming, the activation of judgment heuristics, creating familiarity that offers processing fluency, and shaping the brand memory by creating or reinforcing connections with favorable qualities, capabilities or contexts?

When aiming at the conscious mind makes sense
I have stressed all the way through this book that the nonconscious mind is the key driver of purchase decisions. It follows that you need to focus on the nonconscious mind rather than on delivering 'rational' arguments that engage the conscious mind. However, nothing is ever black and white when it comes to marketing: there are some situations where a more rational approach represents a sound strategy.

Consider what happens when a consumer talks about a brand or product. This is a conscious process and the consumer will rationalize in order to present a more-or-less logical story or assessment. Obviously it is to your advantage to give the consumer a 'script' that they can pick up and use when they talk to third parties. In this way you have a greater degree of control over word-of-mouth and, given the growing importance of social media, this is a key consideration.

There is a classic example that ticks all the boxes: Mercedes, when it was still a leading luxury car that was unaffordable for most, appealed to the nonconscious mind with a prestige and exclusivity message while also stressing the safety aspect as a rational reason for buying. The idea was that you could buy a Mercedes to satisfy your goal of showing that you had arrived financially and socially, while presenting the purchase to others as a means of keeping your family safe.

An important point to always keep in mind is that the nonconscious and the conscious minds each focus on different exposures. The nonconscious will look for cues and signals that allow it to classify the exposure so that it can create a memory and link it meaningfully to other, existing memories. The conscious mind, on the other hand, will seek to understand the message by applying rational thought. It is therefore possible to create communications that delivers 'food for thought' for both minds, but in most instances the focus needs to be on the nonconscious as the driver of the purchase decision.

Creating, shaping and activating memories
First I need to remind you that I am using 'ad' as shorthand for 'touchpoint'. The principles outlined in this section apply regardless of the type of exposure (passive, active or interactive) or media used to deliver it (e.g., traditional broadcast or digital media, including social media).

Second, I need to explain that when I refer to an 'ad memory' I am talking about all of the aspects of your marketing communication that have been placed by the nonconscious mind into the consumer's memory when exposed to it. It is very important to note that this is not the same as the conscious memory the consumer can recall. Rather, the ad memory comprises of elements the consumer can recall, as well as others they can't.

Similarly, a 'brand memory' is a compilation of everything the consumer has placed into memory about your brand, including the connections their mind has made to other, existing, memories. Again, this includes elements the consumer can recall and others they can't.

Unless your brand is new to the consumer, the brand memory has most likely been shaped over a period of time during which the consumer was exposed to a multitude of touchpoints including packaging, logo applications, signage, consumption or usage experiences, observation (seeing others using or consuming the brand) and, of course, any communications touchpoints that have been linked to the brand memory.

There are three challenges here, namely to:
- establish a strong and diverse ad memory
- link the ad memory to the brand memory
- activate the ad memory once it has been established.

Highly effective and cost-efficient marketing communications result from addressing all three challenges.

Creating a strong and diverse ad memory

From a media perspective there are two key criteria: firstly, the intensity and diversity of sensory signals the ad sends; and second, the mood the consumer is in at the time of exposure.

Take a cinema ad, for example: a large screen ensuring high-impact visual images, surround sound for high-impact audio signals and, importantly, an audience that does not perceive the ads as an interruption but waits in anticipation for the feature movie to begin. Or consider the impact of Superbowl ads when many consumers are actually looking forward to the ads because they expect them to deliver entertainment, surprises and delight.

When the consumer is in such an anticipatory mood, or when the ad offers a particularly intense sensory experience, it is much more likely that a strong ad memory will be created. What should be obvious is that the creative content needs to make full use of such sensory opportunities for them to be effective. Obviously, a cinema ad that does not deliver high-impact images or audio is not likely to have the desired impact.

Of course, there is also the issue of reach: for example, when the reach of cinema is not sufficient then trade-offs have to be made between high-impact sensory inputs and other media options that deliver more extensive reach. But, given the importance of creating a strong ad memory in the first place, I would argue that the role of cinema advertising (and other high-impact sensory media) in the media mix deserves to be given attention.

Creating an ad memory that can be activated efficiently and effectively

As your goal is to activate the ad memory as often as you can once it has been established, you should plan ahead and use a diversity of sensory inputs when creating the ad memory in the consumer's mind. Compare, for example, the creation of an ad memory that uses only words, with an approach that also uses images and sound. In the first case you can only activate the ad memory using words, while in the latter case you can also use images, music, a jingle or a 'signature' sound to trigger the ad memory.

Linking the ad memory to existing memories (other than the brand memory)

You may want to not just enrich the ad memory, but also link it to existing – currently unrelated - memory patterns. A simple example is the use of a celebrity many consumers recognize (i.e., have a memory of). By strongly linking the ad memory to such a celebrity you can expect that ad memory to be activated whenever the consumer is exposed to the celebrity. This might provide you with frequent activations outside of the advertising context without paying extra for them.

Or consider an example where you link the ad memory to a key issue, such as the environment. Whenever the consumer engages with environmental issues, reports, discussions, etc., their ad memory may also be activated.

You have to be very careful, however, as there is a risk that the celebrity or broader issue to which you have linked our ad memory may be highly complex ('complex' in this context means the memory is liked to other memories that have no connection to your brand), thus triggering memories that do not benefit your brand. This is typically a problem with sponsorships when there are too many brands sponsoring the same event or team and there is no dominant, differentiating role your brand plays. It may still help you to boost familiarity with your brand, but it is unlikely to have a positive impact on sales due to the focus of your sponsorship or brand endorsement being more strongly linked to other brands or content than to your own.

Linking the ad memory to the brand memory

We have assumed so far that it is sufficient to activate the ad memory – that is, when the consumer is exposed to *fragments* of an ad, their nonconscious activates the whole ad memory. That's fine as far as it goes, but creating an ad memory is obviously only a means to an end, not the end itself. Unless the ad memory is closely linked to the brand memory, your advertising is unlikely to have any impact on your sales.

While this may seem obvious, it is often ignored when developing an ad campaign. Especially when it comes to social media, success is often measured by how many people engage, rather than asking the much harder question of what impact, if any, the exposure is actually having on the *brand memory*.

Experience has shown that a high level of engagement (as measured by likes or views) does not necessarily translate into useful marketing outcomes (such as a more favorable brand image or an increase in market share) if the engagement doesn't bear any relationship to the brand. For example, Budweiser for many years booked millions of viral views related to Bud tv, while the brand's market share continued its slow decline. The Pepsi Refresh campaign I mentioned in an earlier section is another example where generating a high level of engagement had no positive impact on sales.

Unless your brand is central to the engagement or exposure, you risk a situation where there is a strong ad memory but no link, or only a very weak one, to the brand memory. This results in the ad failing to shape the brand memory, i.e., how the consumer thinks and feels about the brand and, ultimately, their purchase decision.

Activating the ad memory once it has been established
Following the guidelines outlined so far means you must take care to:
- link the ad memory with the brand memory, by making the brand the hero or at least an integral part of your communications, highlighting how your brand can address specific, important (nonconscious) goals
- establish an ad memory using diverse sensory inputs, allowing you to activate your ad memory in many different ways (such as using images, or sound, or stories, etc.)
- possibly also link the ad memory in a dominant way with existing, relevant memories (such as celebrities, broader issues, etc.), allowing the ad memory to also be activated whenever these previously unrelated memories are activated.

An important result of this approach is that you need to ensure your communications program creates an ad memory with diverse, high-sensory exposures and to link this ad memory to the brand memory. Once that has been achieved you no longer need expensive, high sensory exposures because you can activate the ad memory, and through it the brand memory, by activating just an element of the now-existing ad memory. So brief exposures that trigger the ad memory are all you require.

Now you get a bonus: whenever the brand memory is activated the consumer's ad memory will also be activated. Whenever the consumer is exposed to packaging, logos, consumption or usage occasions or even just sees other people using or consuming the product, these and other exposures will activate not only the brand memory but also the ad memory you have so carefully crafted. This means consumers will be reminded of the message you have planted in the ad memory: how the brand can address certain goals, the brand's unique qualities or capabilities, and so on.

Finally, keep in mind that links between neurons that get activated together grow stronger, while links that do not get activated become weaker. It follows that frequent activation is an essential contributor to building a strong and diverse brand image.

Understanding and targeting a key driver of brand choice

Marketing communications that do not activate a key driver of brand choice are not likely to have a significant impact. Such an ad could boost familiarity, but it is unlikely to build your brand. Let me explain this problem using a behavioral change campaign as an example. You would think that such a campaign would take extra care to target a key driver of behavior. Unfortunately, that's often not the case.

Consider a campaign that aims at reducing the road toll by shaping driver behavior. We know that one of the biggest problems when it comes to road safety is the widely held belief amongst drivers that they are better than the average driver. This has been extensively documented in research study after research study in a number of countries.

People do know that they can get seriously injured in an accident. That's obvious, as frequent reports in the mainstream media talk about death and serious injury, news and current affairs reports show graphic images of accident scenes, and movies deliver dramatic crashes that cause serious injury (except to the hero, of course, who walks away unscathed). There would be very few people who believe they could be in a major car crash and not face the risk of serious injury.

But this does not prevent them from driving fast, being careless, or driving under the influence of alcohol or drugs. It does not prevent them from doing so because they believe their superior driving skills will ensure that *they* don't have an accident. It is quite common for drink drivers to belief that they are capable of driving safely no matter their blood alcohol level.

It therefore came as a surprise to me that an ad agency developed a major campaign built around 'Graham', a body constructed to withstand a serious accident. Sure, the heavy padding, massive head protection and so on did highlight that human beings are not designed to walk away from a serious accident. But we all know that already. We know that accidents can lead to serious injury or even fatalities. The problem is that we believe we won't have an accident because we are such superior drivers.

In other words, the campaign told drivers something they already know, but which does not have an impact on driver behavior. Perhaps not surprisingly given the advertising industry's general lack of strategic competence, 'Graham' went on become the most awarded advertising campaign in 2017 according to the Gunn report.

What is the answer?

If drivers believe their skills are well above average and thus are able to drive safely even when speeding or using their mobile phone, we can't win by telling them again and again that these behaviors represent serious risks or that accidents can cause serious injuries. They will nod their heads and agree that these are huge problems – except for them, because they are such brilliant drivers.

It follows that we have to change the risk factor to one

that cannot be avoided by being an excellent driver. This has been done successfully by investing into Random Breath Testing (RBT), speed cameras and serious fines. Imagined superior driving skills do not help when it comes to avoiding RBT or speed cameras.

In summary, ad campaigns that emphasize the risk of getting caught and the consequences of that are a much better investment into changing behavior than campaigns that tell drivers that accidents can cause serious injury or death – something they know already and they believe they can avoid due to their superior driving skills.

Unfortunately, the Graham story is by no means unique. The most awarded ad ever is 'Dumb Ways to Die', an ad developed on behalf of Melbourne Trains, using cartoon figures to show that people can die from a wide range of stupid behaviors, such as playing with a hornets' nest, drinking cleaning liquids, taking your helmet off in space or crossing rail tracks when trains are approaching. The outstanding music track did much to encourage tens of thousands of people to like the ad, post comments, upload their own versions, and so on.

My concern was that this ad might actually encourage teenagers to play 'Dumb Ways to Die'. It certainly was not an ad that would encourage safe behavior – it was basically a highly entertaining ad lacking a relevant message. Not surprisingly, the media reported that the safety record during the first six months after the campaign broke was the worst for a decade. Yet this ad – which anyone with just a basic understanding of what drives behavior would surely know was a waste of money – went on to win more awards than any ad ever in the history of advertising.

In the interest of disclosure I should mention that I am guilty of having worked in the advertising industry for quite a few years – for JWT, Clemenger BBDO and Mindshare. I do find this industry exciting but, while there are some notable exceptions, there is a widespread lack of understanding of how to shape purchase decisions.

In the absence of a strategy, focus on familiarity

Familiarity is a key driver of behavior in many choice situations. I also believe, without stretching the concept too far, that even habits are built on a solid foundation of familiarity.

Let's say you have never bought tomato sauce before but want to use a recipe that requires this ingredient. You stand in front of the supermarket shelf and look at a dozen tomato sauce brands (if you are in Italy you may have a lot more than a dozen to choose from!). You may make a choice based on price or pick the most attractive pack – or you may pick the brand that is most familiar. Familiarity provides a feeling of security, of having made a safe choice. It is linked to social validation, i.e., people picking options they believe many others have also selected.

Habits are created by repetition. They are typically triggered by a familiar stimulus or context. For example, driving a familiar car means you can drive virtually on auto-pilot, a familiar bathroom triggers the standard morning ablutions routine without having to think about what to do first or next, a familiar pack facilitates habitual shopping for groceries, et cetera.

I won't explore this further as it is not important for marketers to have a view on the link between habits and familiarity. However, it *is* important to understand that ad campaigns can have a positive impact on consumer choices even if they are quite ineffective in building the brand. The reason: they can boost brand familiarity, and when consumers need to make a choice and there is no particular brand that is expected to address a goal in the consumer's mind, familiarity becomes the dominant driver of brand choice.

My view is that the vast majority of ads are ineffective in building the brand – but this does not mean that they haven't added any value. They can still impact on brand choice by boosting familiarity. Of course, a great ad will provide a reason to buy by convincing the consumer that the brand can address a goal, which is much more effective than just boosting familiarity.

Mood congruency

Clearly, an important goal for marketers is to either create a mood that is conducive to purchase, or to present the purchase opportunity in an environment that does so. This makes positioning your ad in an appropriate TV program or magazine context, and using effective in-store mood management through displays and other sensory inputs, important marketing decisions.

Importantly, environmental factors can impact on moods. For example, interacting with friendly and helpful sales assistants may make you feel valued and put you in a positive mood. In times past, liveried greeters could be found at the door of major U.S. retail outlets, a practice that has just about disappeared. The function of these greeters was to put shoppers into a good mood when entering the retail store by welcoming them and, if time permitted, exchanging a few positive words.

One of the questions of interest to marketers is to what extent the mood created by the media context – for example, the television or radio program, the magazine story, the movie, the location of out-of-home initiatives, the website, or the social network – impacts on the effectiveness of an ad. I expect much more research to be done in this area, but initial results suggest that the impact could be quite significant.

Vizeum Germany conducted a study testing the impact of television ads placed in a 'suitable' and 'unsuitable' television show, with suitability determined by the mood congruency between the product and the show. More specifically, they placed a feminine chocolate ad and a masculine beer ad into, respectively, 'Boston Legal', a fast moving legal drama and 'How I Met Your Mother', a comedy/romance show. Predictably, ads placed in a context that delivered mood congruency were more effective.

Neuro Insights, an Australian firm, researched a number of television programs and a set of advertisements and found that if an ad is in tune with the program's neurostate, it is likely to be more effective. Here, the neurostate was divided into two categories: dominance of emotions versus dominance of cognitive processing.

Essentially this means that an ad that relies largely on cognitive processing (i.e., an ad aiming at engaging the conscious mind) should be placed in the context of a media exposure (a TV program, a magazine article, a website context, etc.) that is likely to get the consumer *thinking* about things, while an ad that aims primarily at activating emotions rather than cognitive processing (i.e., an ad aiming at the nonconscious mind) is more effective when placed in a media context that activates *emotions* in the viewer.

In another study, it was found that a product fit between an ad and the television program's theme increases recall, but an emotional fit lifts recall even further (in this particular study, recall increased by 9% with product fit and by 15% with an emotional fit).

So what are product fit and emotional fit? A product fit would see the ad being placed in a program that fits with the product category; for example, a car ad in a motoring show such as 'Top Gear'. An emotional fit is found when the qualitative aspects of the program and the ad are aligned. For example, if a car ad focuses on the design and beauty of the car, it is more effective when placed in a fashion or home-design program that also focuses on design and beauty.

All this is not unexpected. Media planners have forever looked for some congruency between the media context and the ad. However, the focus was more often on a product fit rather than emotional fit. Neuroscience research suggests that emotional fit is likely to deliver a greater impact and thus a greater return.

Naturally, there are many other considerations such as reach, frequency and cost. It may be very well to think about placing a car ad that focuses on design in a television program or magazine article that explores leading edge design, but it would obviously be useless to do this if potential car buyers are unlikely to view such a TV program or magazine article. In other words, our deeper insights into mood congruency, delivered by neuroscience research, need to calibrate rather than determine media choices.

It's important to understand that mood congruency relates to the fit between the *specific* media context (the program, article, story, video, game, etc.) and the *specific* ad or other exposure. An approach that is simply based on congruency between the overall brand positioning and the positioning of a media property is not likely to succeed in most instances. For example, BMW's positioning may be based on driving pleasure and thus it would seem that using a magazine that is about the pleasure of driving, going on holidays, visiting places, etc., might be a safe choice. But what if the specific ad under consideration is about engineering excellence or beautiful design features, about roominess or off-road capabilities?

The decision must always be made at the level of the specific ad, not the overall brand positioning. You need to ask yourself: Are consumers immersed in this media likely to be receptive to the specific messages we are sending with this ad?

Further, many media options offer a vast range of different content contexts. Open any women's magazine or visit an online chat room and you find contexts as diverse as romance, family, successful mothering, child development, health and fitness, holidays, celebrity gossip, and so on. It is not the positioning of the media asset that is the critical issue here, but the mood a *specific* article or editorial is likely to create.

Digital media
Digital media is really just another communications and engagement channel and much of what we have learned about traditional media also applies to digital. There is,

however, a key difference between a consumer searching and a consumer exploring when using digital media. When searching, consumers typically have a clear objective and are task focused. They are not highly receptive to advertising, unless the ad is directly relevant to their search objective.

When exploring, however, consumers are looking for excitement, surprises and new experiences and are therefore much more receptive to any ads that promise to address these goals.

What makes digital media challenging is the rapid change brought about by innovation. Let me mention a few trends that are already starting to change the current landscape:

Voice
When interacting with a digital assistant one does not have to type or read: it is a verbal discussion. In the not too distant future we will see voice replacing written communications when it comes to interacting with – or via – digital media. Consumers will post comments by dictating them, and will hear rather than read comments and other content, sometimes delivered by video and at other times just by voice.

The widespread use of voice will allow for sizing down gadgets. However, the use of video and images will still require a larger screen. Amazon's screen-based Echo is a great option that facilitates both, allowing the consumer to choose the mode they want.

Artificial Intelligence
AI not only helps you to use programmatic media effectively and to optimize your media schedule and budget, it also has an impact on the consumer's experience. AI and the use of avatars is revolutionizing direct interactions with customers with the potential of providing faster and more accurate information, may this be in a shopping situation or when inquiring or complaining. AI can also assist the consumer when shopping in a behind the scenes role by presenting

relevant items and delivering appropriate comments. AI can control the flow of ads to ensure that only the most relevant ones reach the consumer.

Your own personal drug factory!
Social media can address a wide range of goals, from entertainment to belonging, from exploring to simply trying to keep up with the world. However, many consumers use social media to create a positive image for themselves by trying to gain recognition or respect – for example, by being the first in their social network to find something funny or exciting or important to share, to be seen to achieve or lead, to seem to be having more exciting experiences, eating at better restaurants, being smarter than others, and so forth. These consumers share content to confirm membership in their informal peer group, to chat about the latest gossip, to influence others by posting emotional content or images, and to regulate group membership by supporting those who conform to implicit group rules and punishing others who don't by ignoring their posts.

Social media delivers recognition and rewards. When a consumer receives (positive) messages from 'friends' in social media their brain releases dopamine, the neurotransmitter that makes them feel good. Dopamine release is also triggered by reading their own posts, getting lots of likes, or ending up amassing a large number of 'friends' or followers, to mention just some of the many 'rewards' the internet has in store for us.

It's not hard to see how sharing something on social media triggers a dopamine release. We all have a drive to explore, to belong, to be recognized as particularly good at something, to be successful and to be seen to succeed, and when we can't satisfy these drivers in the real world we can definitely make a show of them online. As we address these goals we get a dopamine release, driving us to address them again, looking for an even stronger and more frequent release.

This opens up a great opportunity: targeting consumers

when they share social content, i.e., online content across all social networks and via Dark Social channels. A clarification of what 'Dark Social' is might be in order at this stage. Dark Social sharing is the copying and pasting of content and links from websites into email or instant message services and selectively sharing it with friends, family and colleagues. Dark Social typically accounts for a significant share of total social sharing. For example in Australia Dark Social sharing is 3.5 times the size of Facebook sharing.

For each Dark Social share, the content and the people it is being shared with are selected for a very specific reason. This is very different to the data collected from public social networks, where sharing centers around what an individual considers suitable for public examination.

Neuroscientists have found evidence that males and females differ in terms of what drives their online behavior. *Males* have higher levels of dopamine and testosterone than females, which characteristically drives them to be more aggressive and self-centerd. As such, men are more likely to display competitive online social behavior. Men also have a stronger drive to explore socially than women, meaning they are less 'safe' in their social sharing behavior. *Females*, on the other hand, have higher levels of oestrogen and oxytocin and feel emotions more intensely than men. They are driven to bond deeply and build strong relationships. Women seek greater 'social intimacy' through their sharing behavior.

It is therefore likely that men are driven to share content through a need to compete – to be seen to be successful or to position themselves as achievers and leaders. Women are more likely to share content that confirms membership of their informal peer group, to chat about the content they are sharing rather than about themselves, and to post more emotion-based content, i.e., they want to belong.

Starting with a small step....
As discussed earlier, mood congruence can boost the impact of your marketing communications. Being aware of what consumers share allows you to align your message when re-targeting them.

But there is another driver at work: Neuromarketing research has shown that people who take a small step are more likely to take a bigger step afterwards. For example, animal shelters find it difficult to adopt out kittens. Uber ran a promotion on National Cat Day, inviting customers to order a 'Kitten Car' through the app. A kitten from a local animal shelter would arrive at the consumer's door to play for 15 minutes. The intentions around the promotion were to activate a fun way to promote feline welfare. However, for those people who took the first step of bringing a kitten into their home or workplace, it increased the likelihood of attachment and, in turn, the successful adoption of a kitten in need. Globally, across all cities, shelters participating in this campaign saw an increase in donations and adoptions.

What this tells us is that taking a first step – regardless of how small it might be – will create an affinity with the event, brand or activity. The consumer becomes more receptive to taking another, bigger step in the same direction.

It makes sense to target consumers who share content that is relevant to your product or service – they are far more likely to be emotionally engaged and receptive to your offer at that time. Sharing opportunities represent the small steps we want consumers to take so that they are more receptive to taking a bigger step – either purchasing or engagement with the brand in a meaningful way.

Speed is critical
Once consumers have shared content, there is an opportunity to directly target them online. We now know when consumers will be most responsive to an offer because they have taken that small step (sharing content

with others who may have the same interests or intentions) and are in the prime emotional state of experiencing a dopamine release.

Research conducted by RadiumOne found that targeted advertising delivered within the first hour after a consumer signals 'intent to buy'[21] results in conversion rates up to seven times higher than in the following hour. This occurs through real-time media buying across social, video, mobile and display channels. Speed is critical when it comes to connecting with relevant consumers in a primed emotional state, wherever they are across the open Web and mobile.

In summary here is how it works. We know that consumers go through a number of phases when they share:
- They experience a dopamine release which makes them feel good about their sharing.
- Not long afterwards, as the released dopamine dissipates, they will feel a desire for another dopamine hit.
- This makes them more receptive to any proposition they hope might deliver a dopamine release (this process takes place in the nonconscious, so consumers are typically not aware of why they are more receptive).
- If the message we are delivering is aligned with the content they shared earlier, we know that they are more open to our offer than consumers who have not shared relevant content.

These basic tips will enable your brand to unlock the value of sharing:
- Make it easy for consumers to share your content and for you to track the activity. Use smart sharing

---

[21] 'Intent' to buy can be signalled by what the advertiser determines is a likelihood to buy, e.g. visiting a site and browsing a specific product or going through to an online checkout but not purchasing, sending a link or content to a product to friends or family.

widgets and URL shortening software on owned media and for all social activity.
- Activate the data gathered from the sharing of your content across all channels, including native content, and ensure that the data is easily actionable for paid media targeting rather than restricted to analytical and reporting purposes.
- Work with providers who can gather and act on social data in real-time. This ensures you are engaging consumers while they are in the 'sweet spot' of receptiveness.
- Gain visibility into *all* relevant social sharing, including Dark Social, enabling you to then connect with those audiences outside of your owned and earned media environments.

Ad-skipping
With a growing number of consumers opting for time-shifted viewing, there has been growing concern amongst marketers and their media agencies about the impact on television advertising. Research shows that not all is lost when consumers skip ads. As long as consumers have had a prior full exposure to an ad, and have therefore had the opportunity to establish a memory of that ad (the 'ad memory'), they don't need to watch the ad all the way through for it to have an impact when they see it in the future.

Several studies have confirmed that even ads seen at high speed are likely to activate the consumer's ad memory, *as long as this memory has already been established* by a prior exposure to the full advertisement. Arguably the most compelling evidence is the classic Du Plessis study that showed that fast-forwarded ads even trigger the emotional elements of the ad memory.

Du Plessis used a cinema environment to conduct his test. He showed ads at triple fast-forward speed and measured recall and liking, which he then compared to Millward Brown's AdTrack system as an independent sample. As we have already discussed, recall is not a true measure of effectiveness, but this study nevertheless delivered some compelling results.

The fast-forwarded ads were recalled by between 40 and 90 percent of the audience, and most people who recalled an advertisement claimed that they had seen the ad before. The cinema liking scores correlated highly with scores given in the independent AdTrack survey. But - in my opinion - the most important finding was that when two funny ads included in the reel where shown at fast-forward speed many audience members laughed. This means they not only recognized the advertisements, they also reacted emotionally to them in the intended way.

I have already stressed that recall and recognition measures are not telling us the full story. Unfortunately, today these are the measures most commonly used by researchers, academics and the marketing fraternity. No doubt as neuromarketing evolves, new measures will be adopted that provide us with more relevant and deeper insights into the impact of communications, media and creative strategies and their execution.

Let me close this section with a couple of observations. When consumers fast forward ads they are typically looking at the television screen because they want to make sure they don't miss the start of the television program they are viewing. In fact, it is not uncommon for ad-skipping consumers to do one or both of the following:
- slow down from, say, a 12x or 6x speed to a 2x speed when they anticipate the end of the ad break is approaching to make sure they don't miss the start of the TV program
- focus even more closely on the screen to ensure they catch the end of the ad break.

A consumer giving full attention to the screen to watch for when the program starts is not distracted by other thoughts – they are not thinking about what to cook for dinner, what snacks are in the fridge, how to deal with the children or an issue at work. Our brains are not designed to multi-task: at the early stage of the ad break they may be thinking about all sorts of things, focusing only now and then on the screen, but towards the end of the ad break they are likely to concentrate almost exclusively on the screen.

This means that ad-skipping viewers actually pay attention - not to the content of the fast-forwarded ad as such, because it is fragmented and they are not actively trying to reconstruct the ad in their mind - but nevertheless they are following closely what is happening on the screen. It follows that there is an advantage in being the last ad in an ad break (or at least placed towards the end of the break).

Multi-tasking
I have mentioned ad-skipping as a major concern. Another concern is multi-tasking, i.e., the consumer engaging with their smartphone, tablet or computer during an ad break.

Before exploring the implications of multi-tasking let me air a gripe of mine: how companies destroy their own markets. Take, for example, the car industry. They apparently were surprised by the dramatic shift to smaller cars and blamed the oil crisis and resulting high petrol prices for this market disruption. But the truth is that car manufacturers started to offer many of the features that had been reserved for top-of-the-line cars in their smaller models, making these suddenly much more attractive. After all, why pay for a more expensive model when you could now get the same safety, entertainment, functional and comfort features in a smaller car?

Or consider retailers who - presumably due to a lack of imagination - have focused on price discounting and now complain that consumers won't buy unless they offer massive discounts. What did they expect would happen when they started to make price their main competitive weapon?

And right now we can see another great example of how an industry is damaging its market: TV channels encourage viewers to multi-task by displaying messages on the screen and encouraging viewers to comment on social media while a program is on. These may be Twitter messages related to the program being watched, ads for other shows or for paying advertisers. The point is that they are engaging the viewer's cognitive mind and training them to multi-task even when they are watching a show of their choice. Clearly, this is likely to encourage many consumers to continue interacting with their smartphone, tablet or computer during an ad break (as well as during programs).

But let me return to the main focus of this section: how advertisers can deal with the multi-tasking challenge.

First, keep in mind that consumers do not in fact truly multi-task: they simply switch from one task to the next. The conscious mind is not designed to multi-task. Not that this makes much difference to what happens: the consumer is engaging with another screen - a mobile phone, computer, or some other device. However, while the *conscious* mind laboriously switches from task to task – from the tablet or smartphone to the TV screen and back again - the *nonconscious* mind is soaking up any signals that are being received, processes them and possibly stores them in memory, often enriching existing memory patterns.

For the most part the sensory inputs are very different to the ones the ad-skipping consumer receives. The ad-skipper does not get any audio, but is exposed to a series of visual images that present a short-hand message. The 'multi-tasker', on the other hand, typically receives fewer visual images but is exposed to the audio, which needs to become the key element of the exposure. This means the audio presents an opportunity to engage the consumer. We may even manage to make them look up and take in more of the ad's message.

For example, when promoting a food product the visual is hugely important as it enables us to activate mirror neurons, which help us to feel what the person we are observing is feeling. When the consumer sees a person enjoying the food in a compelling and emotionally rich way there is a good chance that mirror neurons will be activated. And, when emotions are activated, there is an increased likelihood that the brain will decide to store the experience in memory.

This means that the audio has to deliver a disruption that makes the consumer look up when the critical mirror neuron moment takes place. It also means that, at that point, the brand needs to be visible so it is associated with the positive emotional burst the consumer experiences.

Audio even presents an opportunity to develop a neuro brand signature. When you hear the sound of Windows starting up on your computer you know it is Microsoft. Experiments in liquor outlets have shown that the sound of a cork being released from a bottle and wine being poured into a glass has a significant positive impact on wine sales. What we need to do is create an audio-based neuro brand signature that will activate the brand memory pattern. Jingles that are strongly associated with a brand are a good example for a neuro brand signature. Research has shown that consumers can recall jingles long after they have forgotten the content of ads, and some bars of a jingle can help them retrieve a memory stored by the nonconscious mind.

Finally - an important part of audio is, of course, music and we all know that music can create moods, but it can also surprise, as well as connecting with and activating existing memory patterns.

As with ad-skipping it is likely that ads placed towards the end of the ad break benefit, in this case from the consumer looking up more frequently to ensure they don't miss the start of the program while multi-tasking.

In summary, then, ad-skipping and 'multi-tasking' create a challenge and you need to review your current advertising practices to make sure you are addressing - rather than ignoring - this challenge. But neither of these behaviors is 'killing' the TV ad. It is simply a matter of adapting the way you use the television medium, from a creative as well as a placement point of view.

And, as always, not everything changes. In this new, emerging environment you can expect integrated campaigns to work better than isolated TV ads and you may have to eventually redefine the role of the TV ad within the communications mix. But even then you will want to utilize television as a true mass medium that can give you exposure and can effectively activate an integrated multimedia campaign. Except, you may find that in this scenario television's main role is to reinforce the memories created by other media exposures. For example, if a full-length TV ad is launched and has achieved high exposure, you can activate the ad memory by exposing the subsequent TV audience to just fragments – similar to the signals the minds of ad-skippers or 'multi-taskers' receive.

Ad fraud and ad blocking
Two challenges many marketers face these days are ad fraud and ad blocking. The former is the criminal diversion of marketing funds by generating artificial consumer activity, such as a bot clicking on banner ads or visiting websites. Ad blocking is the consumer's use of ad-blocking software that blocks any digital ads from reaching their screen(s).

Ad fraud
Automated software programs known as bots, the primary vehicle for ad fraud, have infected a range of advertisers. The costs to advertisers are significant. Losses during 2017 due to ad fraud have been estimated at $6.5 billion which is – hard to believe – an improvement over the $7.2 billion reported a year earlier.

A survey of 49 members of the US Association of National Advertisers (ANA) covering activity between October 2016 and January 2017 sheds more light on the impact of ad

fraud.[22] Key findings, showing a marginal improvement during 2017, are:
- *Traffic sourcing is still the major risk factor for fraud.* Traffic sourcing, or the process of purchasing traffic from inorganic sources, was again a large source of fraudulent activity. The report said 3.6 times as much ad-fraud came from sourced than non-sourced traffic.
- *Nine percent of desktop display and 22 percent of video spending was fraudulent.* This was a decline from the previous year when display advertising fraud was reported at 11 percent and the fraud rate for desktop video was 23 percent.
- *Mobile fraud was found to be considerably lower than expected.* Overall, participants saw less than two percent of fraudulent activity in app environments and mobile web display buys. However, this does not include fraud in mobile web video and pay-per-click fraud which remain high and problematic.
- *Fraud in programmatic media buys is no longer riskier than general market buys* as media agencies have improved filtration processes and controls.

Ad blocking

Ad blocking is arguably an even greater challenge for marketers. First, because it demonstrates that many consumers do not want to see the ads that marketers spend millions to develop and deliver to their devices. Second, because ad-blocking has been adopted so widely. In the US around 27 percent of internet users had installed ad blockers according to research firm eMarketer. More specifically:[23]
- 11% of the global internet population is blocking ads on the web
- Ad-block usage grew 30% globally in 2016
- Mobile ad-block usage grew by 108 million to reach 380 million devices

---

[22] *The Bot Baseline: Fraud in Digital Advertising* 2017 ANA Report
[23] For up-to-date statistics visit PageFair's website. PageFair is a leading authority on ad-blocking.

- Desktop ad-block usage grew by 34 million to reach 236 million devices
- 74% of American ad-block users say they leave sites with ad-block walls
- Ad-block usage is now mainstream across all ages.

In a recent move, Google introduced selective ad blocking on Google Chrome, which is used by approximately 60 percent of desktop and mobile internet users. Google has vowed to eliminate the most annoying ads, including video ads that autoplay with sound, pop-up ads with countdowns and 'sticky' ads that take up a large portion of the screen no matter how far you scroll down to try to lose them.[24]

Google bases decisions on which ads to block on the standards set by the Coalition for Better Ads, a group of Internet companies, online advertisers and publishers. Sites failing the 'Google test' have 30 days to improve their advertising standards or the ads will be blocked by Chrome.

This seems a sensible move by Google, given advertising accounted for some 86 percent of Google's $111 billion 2017 revenue. Widespread use of ad blocking by consumers would be catastrophic, so eliminating the most irritating ads pro-actively is a sound strategy. Obviously Google does not want to see ad-blocking software used and the only way to avoid this is to lift the standard of advertising.

Measuring advertising effectiveness

One of the key challenges a marketer often faces is to not only engage the audience of an ad, but to engage them with the brand. Stand-alone engagement measures – like some psychophysiological techniques (EEG or fMRI) – do not tell us whether the viewer is engaging with the brand or rather with the story, talent, visuals or other

---

[24] Hayley Tsukayama, *Google's Chrome ad blocker means the Web's largest ad company is also now advertising's biggest traffic cop*, Washington Post, February 2017

executional elements of an ad.

A Response Time Test can not only answer this question but allows you to evaluate the success of a campaign by highlighting changes in the strength of the connection between your brand and a particular attribute, quality or capability when respondents are exposed to your advertisement. This provides a useful measure in addition to sales, especially in categories with a long purchase cycle.

The following illustration uses a Budweiser TV commercial, assessing if it would actually drive brand choice or would simply create emotional engagement that does not drive purchase decisions.[25]

The results when testing the ad are shown in the following charts:

---

[25] Michal Matukin, *Physiological Measures*, in Paul Dovas, et.al., *Market Research Revolution: A Marketer's Guide to Emerging New Methods*, NMSBA, 2017, pp. 91 ff.

EXPLICIT + IMPLICIT

BRAND B

MOVES ME: 83, 8
IS INFORMATIVE: 60, 20
ENCOURAGE ME TO BUY BEER: 82, 13

CHART DESCRIPTION

OPINION
Explicit & rational

THE BARS - Indicate how many respondents agreed (left bar) or disagreed (right bar) with the statement. The gap between the bars represents undecided respondents.

CERTAIN
Implicit & emotional

THE COLOR CODE - reflects the strength and certainty of an attitude. The higher the speed, the more certain (on average) respondents are about their opinion.

YES: 55 / NO: 20
85 / 8
77 / 13

HIGH CERTAINTY
MODERATE CERTAINTY
LOW CERTAINTY

As can be seen, the vast majority of respondents (over 80%) had positive views, agreeing with the statements *'the ad moves me'*, and *'encourages me to buy beer'* and the majority (60%) declared that the ad *'is informative'*.

However, the implicit Response Time Test shows that while there is a high degree of certainty when it comes to judging emotional involvement (*'moves me'*), there is a high degree of uncertainty when it comes to encouraging purchasing (*'encourages me to buy beer'*). This is a common problem: it is not always clear if the consumer engages emotionally with the brand or with other elements of the ad. Tests that simply show the degree of emotional engagement are typically unable to answer this question.

But what happens to the Budweiser brand perception when consumers are exposed to the Budweiser advertisement? The before and after results are shown in the following charts:

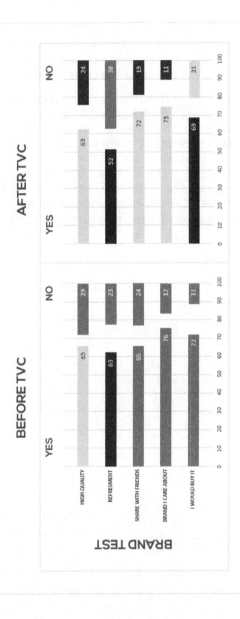

The consumer's memory before being exposed to the TVC shows two things: people truly believe that Budweiser is of *'high quality'* but at the same time there are some issues with the *'refreshing'* value, as it is not perceived as credible. After being exposed to the commercial respondents show more confidence in *'share with friends'* and *'brand they care about'*. It proves that the ad has the potential to convey brand image values and this outcome probably can be perceived as an effect of emotional involvement with the TVC (high scores for *'moves me'*).

Unfortunately, at the same time the ad weakened perceptions of the attribute *'refreshing'*. This attribute already had a slow reaction time in the brand's pre-test and the TV ad did not strengthen it – even explicit answers dropped down in post-test. However, it was the attribute *'I would buy it'* that suffered the most, as respondents' certainty turned from moderate to low after being exposed to the ad.

Clearly, this commercial does not encourage consumers to buy the brand. The ad may positively impact on the brand image but it does not activate a purchase driver.

Advertising and automation

At the time of writing Martin Khin, research VP at Gartner, estimates that the industry is at 10% of the potential for automating the various processes in the advertising sector. However change may be accelerating and Phil Gaughran of McGarryBowen predicted that by 2022, 80% of advertising will be automated. Here are some examples of today's applications:

- *Ad-performance based algorithms*: the placement of an ad is based on its performance. The frequency of high performance ads is increased while low performance ones are switched off.
- *Monetary based algorithms*: sales and conversion data are used to make decisions on increasing or decreasing campaign bids.
- *Predictive advertising*: ReFUEL4 uses artificial intelligence to select an ad for a particular consumer from a pool of different versions the creative team has

prepared. AI uses machine learning to gather data on past performances to learn what works or not for a particular brand. Predictive analysis makes a judgment on the stage of the buying cycle a consumer is in and selects the ad to be sent accordingly.

Here are a few examples of pioneering efforts by agencies and clients:

- McCann Japan created two sets of ads, one made or planned by an AI creative director and the other by a human creative director. The latter was judged as the more effective ad by advertising executives when both were shown at a conference.
- PingGo uses AI to write press releases by asking the clients specific questions and then assembling the answers into content.
- Online logo creators like LogoJoy, Tailor Brands and Withoomph can instantly make logos through the use of browser-based vector graphics software.
- Saatchi & Saatchi LA uses IBM Watson to run different types of AI campaign ads. They match people online with their posted interests to serve ads on behalf of client companies. One campaign for Toyota found people both interested in barbecue and in martial arts. Toyota's agency created an ad called '*taikwan tenderizer*' showing characters using martial arts to tenderize meat for their backyard barbecues.
- AKQA is using IBM Watson to develop a tool that can find potential new audiences online and reach out to them.

13 Shopper marketing and the Path to Purchase

Shopper marketing is an area that has received growing attention during the last decade because it offers an opportunity to impact on the purchase decision at, or close to, the point of purchase. Motivational and associative primes and alert triggers can be effectively used in an on- or off-line retail environment to significantly boost revenues.

However, to fully exploit these shopper marketing opportunities requires integration of all marketing initiatives across the entire path to purchase, and far too often shopper marketing initiatives are developed in isolation rather than being an integral part of a brand strategy and its execution. The following steps are of critical importance if you want your shopper marketing activities to boost your return on marketing investment:

- *revitalize your shopper marketing practice by infusing shopper marketing with neuro insights into how consumers buy*
- *ensure you integrate all key touchpoints, from digital and traditional media to packaging, engagement and interaction opportunities to public relations, brand activation and shopper marketing initiatives*
- *re-focus all marketing activities on the decisive point where the consumer buys – or doesn't buy.*

As I have already discussed, the nonconscious mind plays a dominant role in shaping purchase decisions and is exclusively responsible for habitual purchases.

Most importantly, the nonconscious cannot analyze or make a rational assessment like the conscious mind does. Rather, it takes shortcuts and, being much faster and more powerful than the conscious mind, these shortcuts often have a determining impact on purchase decisions. In identifying these shortcuts the nonconscious mind relies on even minor signals to make sense of an offer.

These shortcuts are called *'judgment heuristics'*. Heuristics are simple rules the consumer's nonconscious uses to make shape behavior. Understanding these rules allows you to influence this process and the resulting outcomes, i.e., the purchase decisions that consumers make.

Not surprisingly, these shortcuts often don't lead to the best decisions. After all, the nonconscious mind has been designed to help us survive by reading cues in the environment and acting on them with speed, not to find the absolutely best washing powder for our laundry needs.

The nonconscious mind either determines the purchase decision directly, getting the consumer to pick an option without any rational assessment, or it primes the deliberate purchase decision by picking up cues that activate memories, goals and judgment heuristics. By tapping into this process – and especially by using priming strategically – you can have a material impact on how the consumer determines meaning and value, which in turn will shape the consumer's experiences and actions, including the purchase decision.

The process of priming is particularly important because it allows you to shape purchase decisions in your brand's favor. Essentially, priming involves leveraging a sensory input that activates associations (related memories) or goals that lead to the nonconscious using judgment heuristics to make the desired decision.

Let me say from the very start that primes are most effective when the consumer is not aware of them. For example, experiments have shown that when a backpack is left in a room people are more co-operative, while a briefcase makes them more competitive. If you were to become aware that you feel in a cooperative mood simply because you saw a backpack, you would most likely fight this feeling as being irrational if not stupid, and by doing so you would minimize the impact of the exposure on your decisions. But when you don't know why you are feeling cooperative you let this mood shape your behavior.

Let me add a few more examples to underline how bizarre human behavior often is:
- Engaging in a game or pursuit that exposes participants to words relating to old age has been shown to prime them to walk more slowly.
- Barely detectable scents of cleaning products can prime hand washing.
- Exposure to a brand can prime behaviors strongly associated with that brand (as we have already seen, exposure to an Apple logo has been shown to prime people to be more creative in a creativity test, while no such priming takes place when people are exposed to an IBM logo).

In many instances consumers are never going to make a rational decision, other than maybe post-rationalizing something they have already done. For example, when a shopper stands in front of a shelf with dozens of yoghurt brands and products she doesn't really want to analyze the offers in great depth, so she is very receptive to a short-cut based on some cue the nonconscious mind has picked up. This might be a Health Foundation tick that endorses a product and is associated in her mind with an unbiased judgment about the nutritional value of the product, or a special price offer, or a flavor that she has enjoyed when buying jam or another type of food product.

You can prime consumers through packaging, marketing communications, pricing, even the environment where the product or brand is offered for sale. You can activate any – and any combination – of the senses, i.e., hearing, smell, touch, sight or taste. Before moving on it is important to differentiate between two different types of priming.

Motivational priming
In *motivational priming* the process triggers a goal and, once that goal is triggered, the mind is receptive to offers that are seen to satisfy that goal. Unlike associative priming (see next section) that has only a short-term impact on behavior, you can expect the goals that have

been activated to lead to purchases and shape purchase decisions over longer periods of time. This makes motivational priming relevant to marketing activities during all phases of the path to purchase – from early exposures to an advertising campaign right up to the point where the purchase is made.

Additional exposures to the sensory inputs that primed the consumer and triggered a goal can reinforce the motivation to buy. This is typically achieved through repeat exposures to advertising and other marketing communications, leading right up to shopper marketing initiatives at the point of purchase. Obviously, these exposures have to consistently activate the same goal to keep motivation high.

There are two caveats when it comes to goal activation: First, when the consumer comes across a way of addressing a goal you have activated that does not involve your brand, they are likely to take advantage of this option and the goal will disappear. Second, you can only activate a goal that already exists in the consumer's mind. If a consumer is not interested in healthy food you cannot activate a healthy food goal, and if you do present your brand as being highly effective in addressing a 'healthy food' goal you will find that consumer unresponsive. However it is possible to convince consumers that your brand can address an existing goal it has not been seen to address in the past.

Here are some illustrations of motivational priming:
- Half of the customers looking to buy a computer in a store were asked about their memory needs, and the other half about their processor-speed needs. The group that was asked about their memory needs ended up buying computers with larger memory, and those in the other group ended up buying computers with higher processor speeds. Getting them to think about certain attributes of the product affected their decision in favor of that attribute.

- The following example is from *Behavioral Economics for*

Dummies[26]: Car ads and product launches at major car shows sometimes use attractive women. Altman suggests that *'the brain processes information in such a manner that people are influenced more by the frame or context within which the car is presented ... than by the substance of the vehicle itself. The argument would be that people are willing to buy the car with the best frame or pay more for the car with the best frame. This suggests that the mechanics of the car matter less than the pretty woman and the environment that frames the car.'*

However, it is important to stress that consumers are unlikely to buy a car they would not want in the first place. *'Your choices are affected by the frame, but the frame doesn't induce you to purchase a vehicle that you wouldn't otherwise want to buy'*, says Altman.

- Car buyers end up buying more options if they start with a fully loaded model and remove options they *don't* want, as opposed to starting with a no-options model and adding the options they *do* want. This is usually referred to as the endowment effect, which leads people to value what they *already* have more than what they *may* get.

- Loss aversion is another judgment heuristic. Offers expressed in terms of avoiding losses — such as 'limited time only' offers — are more likely to be accepted than the same offers expressed in terms of achieving gains.

- Social validation strategies suggest that a majority of other people buy a particular brands or act in particular ways simply because many others do so. Even just putting a shelf-sticker saying that a particular grocery brand is the No.1 brand (i.e., preferred by the majority of other shoppers) can have a significant impact on sales.

---

[26] Morris Altman, *Behavioral Economics for Dummies*, Wiley, 2012

Associative priming
Associative priming creates only a short-term connection between a prime and the memories that trigger certain preferences or behavior. I have already referred to the study which found that people exposed to an Apple logo will be more creative when participating in a creativity challenge than people who have been exposed to an IBM logo.

But as you can imagine, this boost in creativity does not last for long. This is why the prime and the task showing the effect of the priming typically follow each other when experiments of this nature are conducted. Associative priming can be very effective in a shopper marketing context when the purchase is imminent, but would of course be quite ineffective when you expose consumers to an ad and hope for an impact much further down the track.

Here are some examples of associative priming[27]:
- One of my favorites: a UK supermarket placed four French and four German wines, matched for wine style and price, on their shelves. A sound system on top of the shelving unit played French music on even days and German music on odd ones. On French music days 77% of the wine purchased was French and on the German days 73% German.

- Why? This intervention changes the context of the decisions, and the people making the decisions are unlikely, even unable even, to admit the influence of such an intervention. Even when probed if the music had any influence on their purchase decision, 86% of shoppers categorically denied being influenced in any way by the music played.

- Many used cars are sprayed with a fragrance that is similar to the characteristic smell of a brand new car. This smell primes potential buyers, who are likely to rate the used car far more favorably than

---
[27] These examples are taken from Stephen J. Genco, Andrew P. Pohlmann and Peter Steidl, *Neuromarketing for Dummies*, Wiley 2013

they would have without the 'new car smell.'
- A scent of lemon in a restaurant – too weak to be detectable by patrons – is likely to lead to an increase in seafood orders, but only in cultures where seafood is often served with a slice of lemon.
- When consumers were in line to pick up either yogurt or fruit, half of them were asked how they felt about yogurt, and the other half were asked how they felt about fruit. Just talking to them this way greatly biased their decision about what to eat.
- In fast-food restaurants, the introduction of extreme food sizes (for example, five-patty hamburgers) has been found to increase the choice of slightly less 'supersized' options (such as three-patty hamburgers) by providing a new anchor point that makes the previously most extreme option seem less excessive.
- A similar logic is often used in pricing, where an anchoring effect is created by including an extremely high-priced alternative in the consideration set, thereby making alternatives that were previously viewed as expensive appear more moderately priced in comparison. Warehouse stores often use the technique of conspicuously displaying high-priced items like large-screen TVs and jewelry at the front of the store to reduce resistance to purchasing less expensive items elsewhere in the store.
- Similarly, supermarkets tend to put their fruit and vegetable section immediately after the store entrance. Research has shown that consumers buy more packaged goods, including items they know are not good for their health, once they have done the right thing and bought some fruit and vegetables.
- Wine seems to be a favored focus of priming tests. There is a multitude of tests that show that consumers value wine more when it is believed to cost more. Said differently, the price is priming the

consumption experience.

- When a placebo was tested against Prozac but sold at a higher price ($2.50 per pill) than Prozac ($2.00 per pill) it was found that the placebo outperformed Prozac.
- Students were asked to solve as many puzzles as they could. To help them with this task they were offered a caffeine and sugar-rich drink. Half of the group was charged the full price of the drink, while the other half enjoyed a significant discount. The group that got the discounted drink solved 30% fewer puzzles! Again, numerous studies have consistently shown the same result.
- The apparent origin of wine affects the perception of a restaurant's food and even the probability that customers will return. This is called the spill-over effect.
- In an experiment conducted by Cornell professors Brian Wansink and Collin Payne, a group of diners in an Illinois restaurant were served a free, cheap glass of the same Cabernet Sauvignon with the same fixed-price French dinner. However, half were told the wine came from California and the other half North Dakota. The former group not only rated the wine higher, but also the food. They also ate 11 percent more food and were more likely to make a return reservation.

Priming triggers judgment heuristics that allow the consumer to avoid thinking when making purchase decisions by resorting to a shortcut that saves energy and time. The resulting decisions are typically irrational and unlikely to lead to the best outcomes – but they are nevertheless predictable. When activating judgment heuristics in the consumer's mind we find that a majority of consumers behave the same way. This means that judgment heuristics are of strategic value and need to be considered when developing a brand strategy.

Alert triggers
Alert triggers slow down or stop consumers who are

often on automatic pilot while doing their shopping. They are most effective when they signal danger or obstacles in the consumer's way. For example, Woolworths Australia had a great back-to-school initiative in which road signs typically seen near schools were placed in the supermarket aisle where the back to school items were displayed. These signs made shoppers slow down, getting them to give attention to the offer.

Alert triggers do not have to activate goals or create associations with the brand or product on offer to be effective. They simply get more consumers to slow down or stop where your product is being displayed, which should impact your sales favorably.

Expectation management
Managing expectations effectively is an important marketing challenge. For example, promoting excellent service creates high expectations, and these expectations are the reference point against which the consumer will judge the experience. Typically, organizations that aggressively promote excellent service find that consumers have such high expectations that even perfect service doesn't create a positive emotional relationship with the brand.

What is more effective is to keep expectations at a moderate level in order to be able to exceed them, delivering a surprise. It is near impossible to surprise a consumer who has extremely high expectations, and surprise is a necessary pre-requisite to creating a memorable service occasion.

Given these challenges, it is no wonder that expectation management has become an important part of marketing practice. Great marketers understand that it is not only the experience consumers have with the product or service that determines how they feel about and judge their encounter with the brand, but also their expectations.

Of course, what is or isn't a great experience depends very much on how a particular experience stacks up against an individual's past experiences, i.e., relevant memories stored in the mind.

For example, black-and-white television had a signifycant impact when it was launched, but today would have little if any appeal. Similarly, what young people used to find exciting a generation ago is very different to what young people find exciting today, because today's youth are exposed to many more dynamic experiences on a daily basis, and this has changed what they see as exciting.

The same principle applies to day-to-day exposures and the development of expectations. When you can withdraw money from an ATM within seconds, you may find waiting in the bank branch for ten minutes annoying. However, if you live in a developing country and are used to waiting several hours to conclude a simple transaction, you may find a ten minute wait in a bank a highly positive experience.

New experiences and their particular sensory inputs can lead to a *re-classification* of old memories and can also change the impact that future sensory inputs will have. This is fundamental to any brand strategy.

But we need to broaden our horizons even further. So far, we have only considered direct alternatives or competitors (e.g., ATM versus branch banking). Clearly, consumers don't consider products and brands within narrow, logical classifications. In fact, a brand competes with any other means consumers see as being effective in addressing their goals, which may include:
- brands in the same product category
- brands in different product categories
- activities not related to any brand.

Even if the brands and activities offer very different products or services, they could nevertheless address the goal the consumer wants to satisfy, such as to experience:
- fun
- excitement
- being cared for

- friendship
- relaxation
- indulgence
- recognition
- solving a specific functional problem.

The question for the consumer is: 'How can I address my goal?' If, say, the consumer seeks fun and excitement, then your brand competes with all other affordable and available brands and activities that offer fun and excitement, not just with brands that compete in the same product category. It follows that expectations are not necessarily set by the products and brands competing in the same category. There may be products and brands in other categories that determine the consumer's expectations by serving as a standard.

The a-symmetrical world we live in

Consumers tend to give less attention to positive experiences than to negative ones. There are two reasons for this:

First, our nonconscious mind is designed to increase our chances of survival in a hostile environment. In such an environment, it is more useful to remember negative experiences. This allows us to deal with similar experiences more effectively should they arise in the future.

Positive experiences like watching a beautiful sunset or eating some delicious food, however, are not critical to survival. Hence, our brain is designed to store more powerful memories when we experience something negative than when we experience something positive. This is why many people recall the bad things that have happened in their life more easily than the many good things.

The second reason we give less attention to positive experiences is that we can correctly expect a certain experience to deliver predictable benefits that allow us to address our goal(s), so there's no reason to pay much attention until something goes wrong.

This applies to expectations related to many products or brands. Consumers don't look at their car tyres every day and praise them for their performance, not even under the most trying conditions. As long as the tyres work, they are given no further thought. Should the tyres fail, however, consumers will suddenly become strongly interested in their quality and blame the brand for any lack of performance. The same applies to a wide range of functional products and services such as search engines, online banking, electronic equipment, water and electricity supplies, and so forth.

We call this the a-symmetrical world: when things work, consumers don't pay attention; when things *don't* work, they become emotionally involved and create a strong, negative memory.

An interesting point that needs to be given attention, particularly by the service industry, is the question of where the tipping point is. Consider, for example, the queue at a supermarket checkout or retail bank counter. The consumer will give little attention to waiting time when it is short but will get involved emotionally when the waiting time is perceived to be excessive. But at what point does the experience change from neutral and low involvement to negative and high involvement?

Bank of America found that customers waiting for up to three minutes underestimated their waiting time, while those waiting for more than three minutes grossly overestimated their waiting time and developed strong negative emotions. Importantly, the frustration generated by the waiting time will prime the consumer to interpret all sorts of experiences with the bank in a negative way. The bank will find itself on a downward spiral where the negative emotions will distort perceptions.

Getting it all right will – over time – reduce and finally eliminate the negative associations. However, these associations won't be replaced by positive ones. Getting everything right will, in most instances, simply mean that service will be deemed as acceptable rather than exceptional or superior.

Why shopper marketing is so important

While you may agree with the points made so far you may wonder why I see shopper marketing as central to future marketing efforts.

The most compelling reason for my proposition is the need to focus on the *decisive point,* that is, where the purchase decision is being made or where habitual buying determines the choice of brand. But there is another reason for placing an emphasis on shopper marketing: the shopping experience will have a determining impact on the shopper's decision to either delegate the task to a digital personal/home assistant or to shop themselves – may this be online or in a bricks & mortar store. When the shopper expects the experience to be less than rewarding and engaging they are likely to delegate the task, and when that happens there is a fair chance that they will not ask for a specific retail outlet and/or brand to be bought.

It follows that between today and the time when a significant number of shoppers use digital personal assistants, you have to develop an exciting and rewarding shopping experience consumers want to repeat.

Finally it is very likely that in the long-run a significant number of shoppers will be under severe financial pressure, assuming your government introduces the Universal Basic Income at a level well below the average income. This will make it even more important for the emotional relationships that are being built between shoppers on the one hand and retailers and brands on the other to be strong enough to create a desire in the shopper to personally engage.

This suggests that all marketing initiatives need to ultimately focus on the decisive point: they may use primes (in advertising, social media campaigns, etc.) that can be activated at the decisive point; they may build emotional connections that can be triggered at the decisive point; or they may create dopamine hits that can be repeated at the decisive point. Shopper marketing needs to become the starting point for the development of a marketing campaign, rather than the afterthought it so often is today.

Here are some likely developments due to the less than favorable future we have to prepare for:

Retailers and brand owners will increasingly collaborate to create exciting and rewarding shopping experiences.
For retailers there are two core strategies: either offer (only) homebrands or collaborate with the most important brand owners (i.e., the most important to their retail business) to develop an engaging and rewarding retail environment that will benefit both the retailer and the brand owners contributing to this effort.

For brand owners there are also two core strategies: either develop strong emotional relationships with consumers, increasing the chances that they will specify your brand even when delegating the shopping task to a digital personal assistant; or make your brand an integral part of an engaging shopping experience, developed in collaboration with a retailer.

Retailers will complement run-of-the-mill online catalogue type stores with exciting and rewarding store concepts that engage shoppers and bring them back, again and again.
Catalogue stores are typically about convenience, although there are categories (such as fashion, furniture, and interior decoration) where the online store can deliver much more, such as augmented reality applications that allow the shopper to see the product in use.

However, alternatives to a catalogue store need to be offered in categories where such value-added features are difficult to find or where repeat purchases are common. This will allow shoppers to opt either for the rewarding shopping experience or for convenience. Naturally, convenience-focused shoppers are more likely to end up delegating the whole shopping exercise to their digital personal assistant, so developing the reward-seeking shopper is essential when preparing for the future.

Brands will shift more of their spending to in-store shopper marketing initiatives.

Research has shown that consumers are more responsive to ads when they are in shopping mode. This is due to the goal(s) that are activated at the time: when on social media they seek interaction and recognition; when searching they seek answers; when shopping they seek great ideas, innovative solutions, exciting opportunities and new news, making them receptive to promotional messages.

Given that shopper marketing is the decisive point where a brand succeeds or fails and that the shopping environment needs to become much more engaging and rewarding than it is today, it makes sense for brand owners to shift more of their marketing budget from mass media (including social media) to shopper marketing initiatives.

Gamification concepts will be designed to overcome ad fraud and ad blocking, allowing marketers and retailers alike to get their message across.

Gamification can turn the shopping experience into a positive and rewarding one. When the cues that power the gamification concept replace overt advertising we will see many shoppers welcoming these messages about brands and products rather than attempt to block them. And initiatives of this nature are typically also unaffected by ad fraud.

Consultants, communications and shopper marketing agencies will adopt a shared focus, resulting from an integrated approach and true collaboration.

We will see a much greater integration across different facets of the marketing universe. The integrated path to purchase has been elusive, mainly because of the lack of a shared focus. As more brand owners start to focus on the decisive point they will find that integration is not difficult when all touchpoints are focusing on how to influence the purchase decision at that point.

The current obsession with Zero, First, Second, et cetera Moments of Truth and the emphasis on attribution will become somewhat superfluous, as a shared focus will permit assessment of the combined impact of a set of initiatives that have a defining impact at the point of purchase.

Before moving on I want you to think back to the Global Financial Crisis. In some ways it is a long time ago, but does it really feel like a full ten years have passed since the events in 2007 started the crisis? The time ahead of us always seems longer – ten years may seem like a lifetime. You may agree with (some of) my points, but feel that there is plenty of time to take action later. After all, you are extremely busy right now. But look back ten years and you will realize how quickly time passes.

The events we are anticipating will take a few years to play out. Ten years may be an appropriate planning horizon, although the impact of the technological disruption will be felt earlier. Whatever you do, don't fall into the trap of thinking that this gives you plenty of time to get ready for this new and different operating environment. To succeed you really need to start today.

Shopper marketing and automation
Amazon's Alexa, embedded in the Echo speaker and Fire TV players as well as in some cars and household appliances, has taken the lead in the race for market share in digital home/personal assistants. According to *Internet Retailer* Amazon had a 70% share of the US smart-speaker market in 2017, followed by Google with 23%.

Here are some examples of companies that have established a link allowing shoppers to buy their offer via Alexa[28]:

---

[28] Alexa Leads the Charge into Voice Shopping, by Patrycja Malinowska, shoppermarketingmag.com, posted 02/08/2018

- Best Buy lets its customers order its 'Deal of the Day' products via Alexa-enabled devices.
- Sears syncs its full line of Kenmore Smart Appliances with Alexa, letting users control the appliances with a voice command.
- Peapod lets users employ Alexa to add items to their weekly grocery carts in real time.
- Beiersdorf launched an Alexa skill that guides users to the best Eucerin product for their skin.
- Coty's new visual skill, designed specifically for the Echo Show, offers occasion-based look planning as well as visual 'how to-s' and quick tips with recommended products from Coty brands. Products can be directly added to Alexa shopping lists.
- Clorox offers a housekeeping assistant skill that lets users receive product offers via email.
- Unilever's Hellmann's and Best Foods offer a recipe skill.

Amazon is encouraging developers to bring Alexa to more devices while tasking them with building more and better Alexa skills. 'There are now over 30,000 skills from outside developers [and] customers can control more than 4,000 smart home devices from 1,200 unique brands with Alexa,' says Jeff Bezos, Amazon's founder and CEO.

Meanwhile Google has secured alliances with major retailers including Walmart, Target, Costco and Home Depot and it is anyone's guess to what extent Apple, Samsung, Alibaba and others will be able to capture market share.

Amazon and Google capture billions of dollars in advertising spend and not surprisingly, the race is on to find subtle ways to advertise on a digital assistant. A screen obviously helps as consumers are used to having ads served alongside relevant information. But when it comes to voice-only the challenge is much greater. Amazon seems to have found a low-key, but potentially highly effective, approach. When asked to buy toothpaste Alexa might respond (according to a CNBC report): *'Okay, I can look for a brand, like Colgate. What would you like?'*

While digital assistants are changing the way consumers shop, there are technological advances that change the way brand owners and retailers develop and implement shopper marketing programs and how consumers buy.

Artificial Intelligence allows you to:
- time store visits and generate to-do lists for sales representatives based on the different requirements of a particular site
- use image recognition or speech to text technology to save the sales representatives time
- analyze patterns in big data, for example establishing the return on marketing investment and making recommendations on promotional programs.

Here is what some of the pioneers are doing:
- Knorr is using IBM Watson to help customers discover different kinds of food that fit their flavor preferences.
- Whisk.com targets and advertises your products in specific recipe pages.
- Coca-Cola launched an in-store display system that can communicate with the data on a shopper's smartphone. The in-store display can then provide personalized messages when the smartphone owner approaches the display. The system is powered by Google Cloud and the ads are served using DoubleClick's technology.
- Coca-Cola is also using their refrigerated coolers to deliver ads. The coolers are powered by Microsoft. Anhueser-Busch rolled out 1,000 similar displays in sports and entertainment venues, and in convenience stores.
- SwiftIQ is using beacons to deliver personalized messages to smartphone owners when they are inside retail stores. Such messages can be in the form of coupons, recipes or other types of content to encourage the shopper to make a purchase.

Towards an integrated path to purchase approach
Marketers fight many battles: they launch product variations and innovative new products, create

advertising campaigns using traditional and digital media, engage in price and other promotions, offer consumers opportunities to interact, stage competitions, fund sponsorships, develop shopper marketing campaigns, and so on. These and other activities may add up to a market share gain or solidify the brand's current position. But what should the focus be?

To clarify my question let me resort to Baron Antoine Jomini and Von Clausewitz, respectively, who were recognized warfare strategists at their time.[29]

Jomini suggested you win a battle when you have greater force than your enemy at the *objective point*, i.e., the point that has traditionally been identified as being critical to success. Von Clausewitz, on the other hand, believes that we should not try to identify an objective point, which is simply applying conventional thinking to a new challenge. Rather, he advocates that we should seek the *decisive point* – the point where we believe we can win the battle, regardless of where it may be or what conditions it may be fought under.

For example, the traditional approach in your category may be to outspend your competitor. Von Clausewitz, on the other hand, would look for the decisive point and the decisive point is where the consumer makes the purchase decision. This is the point where you have either been successful or failed. There is no point in having an advertising campaign that is effective in making consumers feel positive about the brand or saying that they will buy – if there is no impact on sales.

It would be great if more marketers would take a Clausewitz approach and focus on the decisive point: Are more consumers buying? What is happening at the point of purchase? This is where we need to win the battle. It is not a matter of what consumers say they think they might do or how they feel about a marketing initiative, it

---

[29] William Duggan, *Strategic Intuition: The Creative Spark in Human Achievement*, Columbia Business School Publishing, 2013

is not about consumers engaging with your initiatives, it is about making a sale!

One of the key problems is fragmentation. Large marketing organizations use specialist agencies for digital, social, mobile, creative advertising, media, design and so on. Each of these agencies focuses only on their particular area of expertise and interest – after all that's *their* decisive point, i.e., where their sales are made. And typically these agencies are mirrored within the marketing organization, with specific staff allocated to these respective areas as well. And again, success with respect to the specific areas they are responsible for – rather than the overall impact of the marketing program – is *their* decisive point, i.e., where their career is made or broken.

Naturally, then, each agency or staff expert wants to measure what they are responsible for, arguing that sales are determined by many factors they have no control over. This would be a valid argument if marketing activities worked in an additive fashion. But they don't. They work in an integrated way.

Let's attempt to shed some light on the approach a marketer might take when following Clausewitz' advice to focus on the decisive point, i.e., where the sale is made or lost. First, you need to ask yourself how you can make a sale. There are a number of specific ways of doing so:

- You can attract consumers and get them to habitualize their purchases.
- You can convince consumers who go through a considered purchase decision that your brand addresses their goal better than other brands.
- You can induce impulse buyers to buy your brand.

In each scenario you will face competition, and you may aim at taking market share from competitors and/or to attract newcomers into the market or consumers looking for change. As you already know, the key to achieving this is to:

- activate a goal and position your brand as addressing this goal

- focus on a goal that is already active and position your brand as addressing this goal
- prime the consumer to buy your brand
- use alert triggers to stop the consumer or slow them down while browsing the store or doing their shopping.

The key contribution of advertising, social media, sponsorships, competitions and any other marketing initiative is *to prime the consumer to buy*; to position the brand as a means of *addressing a goal*; to *activate such a goal* encouraging the consumer to buy your brand to satisfy this goal.

Now consider the following: You can use package design, advertising, social media, sponsorships, competitions and other marketing initiatives to create brand assets as well as other associations that are strongly associated with your brand and thus can be triggered at the point of purchase. You can embed primes in the consumer's mind that can be triggered at the point of purchase. You can activate goals that can be addressed at the point of purchase. You can convince the consumer that your brand can address goals it has not previously been seen to address and, again, you can then offer a means of addressing these goals at the point of purchase.

If you focus on how you can truly move the consumer down the path to purchase by working backwards from the point of purchase you end up with an integrated marketing program.

There are, however, some pre-requisites.

First, brand teams and their agencies need to understand how primes can be embedded in the consumer's mind and how they can be triggered. More specifically, they need to understand how associative and motivational priming works.

They have to focus on building brand assets, i.e., qualities or attributes that are distinct and strongly associated with the brand. These are sensory touchpoints such as a jingle, a dominant brand color or a key design element.

These brand assets need to be created in a way that allows for their activation at the point of purchase. In other words, to serve as associative primes.

When you engage via social media you gain little by having consumers just engage with your initiative. Again, you need to embed primes, you need to activate goals your brand can address, you need to position your brand as addressing key goals, you need to reinforce activated goals, et cetera. Most importantly, you need to link any attractive engagement opportunities to your brand, i.e., you need to create a strong and meaningful link between the brand memory and the engagement memory. This typically can only be achieved when you give the brand a central role in the context of the engagement opportunity.

Developing an Integrated path to purchase is no longer a desirable but elusive goal, even for marketers with a diverse marketing mix employing a range of specialist agencies. What has been missing in the past has been a clear and shared focus based on a foundation of factual data. Each key initiative has typically been evaluated in its own right using measures that do not tell us much, if anything, about the impact of this initiative on sales. And brand health tracking and similar efforts to assess progress are often based on irrelevant measures that bear little relevance to sales.

This simple change in focus leads to a massive change in our understanding of the role of advertising, social media, sponsorships, competitions, package design, product innovation and even research methodologies.

The essential, shared marketing task is to embed motivational primes in the consumer's mind that can be activated at the point of purchase; to create brand assets and distinct features that can be used for associative priming at the point of purchase; to activate goals in the consumer's mind your brand is seen to address at the point of purchase; and to convince the consumer that your brand can address goals that have not previously been associated with your brand.

14 Packaging design

In many categories packaging simply protects a product up to the point of purchase and is discarded once the product has been unpacked. This does not mean that packaging is not important. We know that expectations generate dopamine and unpacking a just-bought product is likely to be exciting, making the consumer receptive to messages that can be displayed on the packaging. However, the potential impact of packaging is much greater when it comes to, say, grocery items that stay in their packaging.

With grocery items that are used regularly the consumer is exposed to the packaging far more often than they are likely to be exposed to advertisements for the brand. It follows that packaging is a major channel that can repeatedly expose the consumer to meaningful messages that shape the brand's positioning in the consumer's mind. In the following section I will primarily focus on brands where packaging can make a significant contribution.

Neuroscience research has shown that package design offers the marketer much greater opportunities than previously thought. More specifically:
- Visual elements are processed much more quickly than words, so that visual elements are often responsible for creating engagement, interest and framing the context within which the words are interpreted.
- Visual elements are key to pack recognition, which in turn facilitates habitual buying.
- Because visual elements are key to recognition they also lend themselves to creating brand assets - distinct visual elements that eventually become a short-hand for the brand, such as the Nike 'Swoosh'.
- Visual elements and design features can create a mood that impacts on how the brand and product are received.
- Associative primes can be built into the design to impact on the perceived product qualities and to shape the consumption experience.

- Depending on the product under consideration, design may be able to boost dopamine release at the critical stage of consumption. For example, peeling off the foil lid of a yoghurt container with the intention of eating the yoghurt generates the highest dopamine release (because of the consumer's expectation that they will have a rewarding experience). A meaningful design feature can therefore be used on this lid to connect the brand more closely with the positive dopamine experience, or to assist in developing a brand asset or symbol that can be used elsewhere in marketing communications.
- Motivational primes can be built into the design, leading to the activation of goals.

Of course, a package design needs to be distinct (to aid pack recognition and brand association) and meaningful (to advance the brand story) and to create positive emotions – but as the above examples show, there is so much more design can do.

Purchase behavior – habitual or deliberate?

Many grocery purchases are habitual in nature, i.e., consumers tend to settle on a brand and product variant that is then habitually bought in future, without giving the purchase any attention. This does not mean they buy only one brand. They may have developed heuristics or rules, such as buying a particular brand for:
- children and another for adults (parents)
- everyday use and another when having guests
- cooking and another brand for eating as is
- a certain flavor variant and another brand for another flavor variant.

The point is that in habitual purchasing consumers do not make a deliberate purchase decision, but reach for the familiar brand they habitually buy – either all the time or for a specific purpose or use.

To make matters more complex, some consumers may have habitualized some purchases but not others. For example, they may habitually buy the same cheese for everyday use, but when they expect guests they move into a deliberate purchase decision, exploring different options. A deliberate purchase is particularly likely when dealing with consumption occasions that are only occasional, as habits only form when behavior is repeated regularly.

A package refresh can disrupt habitual buying when you replace the key elements that served as visual cues, i.e., the very elements that allowed the consumer to identify the product they usually buy. This means that you need to understand to what extent your brand relies on habitual buying. If a significant share of your revenue comes from habitual purchases you have to be careful when it comes to a package refresh: if you disturb habitual buying you will almost certainly lose some, and possibly quite a large number, of your current customers.

There are numerous case studies that illustrate the potentially devastating effect of package redesigns. It doesn't matter if the new design is more attractive or highlights the attributes the brand wants to communicate more effectively than the old design. *Without ensuring nonconscious pack recognition you are destroying the habitual buying of your established customer base – and you will pay for that!*

Consider the case of Tropicana fruit juice, a Pepsico brand that achieved number 1 position in many European markets as well as in the US. In 2009 a packaging redesign put a stop to Tropicana's success, resulting in a 19 percent market share loss in key European markets and Pepsico losing some 30 million Euros within a couple of months. Tropicana reverted to its old packaging design at the end of this period to stem the continued sales decline.

In 2012, however, Tropicana successfully revitalized its range – this time making sure to not destroy the original design elements that aided habitual buying and expressed the core product quality (fresh, unadulterated orange juice) – but rather changing packaging format from cartons to plastic bottles. This is a great example of how revitalizing a brand through incremental changes that preserve the key recognition elements can succeed, while also providing a warning to any brand owner who considers making radical changes to their pack design.

Of course, when you are launching a *new* brand you will want to disrupt the habitual buying of existing category consumers, as you can only benefit by such disruption while your competitors are likely to suffer market share losses. Similarly, if you manage a brand that has a very small market share you may benefit from a dramatic new design solution that disrupts habitual buying, as the opportunity to gain share from competitors may by far outweigh any potential losses from upsetting the habitual buying of your brand.

In summary, you need to make a strategic decision on what the design solution needs to accomplish:
- to continue to facilitate habitual buying of your brand – which means you have to preserve any elements of your current design that are critical to pack recognition
- to break category conventions, upsetting as much as possible habitual buying in this category – which means you want a truly innovative design that is distinct and represents a step forward in design development *in the category*, not just for your brand.

Option 1: Incremental improvement by adapting existing designs and logos
This is the right approach when your brand is bought habitually by a significant number of consumers and you don't want to disrupt their buying habits.

When consumers buy habitually, they select the product they usually buy on the basis of package recognition. In other words, without thinking or actively making a purchase decision they simply pick the familiar brand from the shelf or out of the cooling cabinet.

Naturally, when the package is redesigned and the key elements that aided package recognition disappear, the consumer is unlikely to find the brand/product they usually buy and is thus forced to look for alternatives. This turns the thus-far habitual purchase that favored your brand into a deliberate purchase decision, which ultimately may no longer result in your brand being chosen.

Incremental change needs to focus on:
- First and foremost, preserving (sufficient) key elements of the package that aid nonconscious pack recognition to facilitate continued habitual buying by your customers.
- Second, to incrementally introduce new elements or shape existing elements that are consistent with the brand vision archetype you want to bring alive.
- Third, to build motivational and associative primes into the package design that you can trigger as the consumer moves down the path to purchase, especially associative primes you can trigger in the shopping environment.

Usually, it is not difficult to identify the elements of a package design that aid pack recognition – distinct colors, patterns, images and/or layouts are likely to play a part. Remember that the mind is looking for patterns, i.e., visual elements. Words are typically not important as such, but sometimes they are a key visual element of a design solution.

Option 2: Adapting the symbol over time
Just to clarify: the logo is the brand name, i.e., the word, while the symbol is a graphic design solution that is typically connected with the logo. The symbol plays an important role: to ensure continuity you will also have to consider incremental rather than disruptive changes to your logo or symbol.

There are many case examples that show how logos and symbols have been changed incrementally over time to ensure that familiarity is not diminished, while updating the design solutions that would otherwise have started to look faded. Just spend a coffee break googling logo evolution, select 'images' on the Google menu and go through the more interesting examples.

With Bacardi, for example, it was a matter of updating the symbol that was a dominant element of the brand's visual identity. The evolution of the Pepsi logo and its associated color scheme shows how Pepsi changed one element at a time: when there was a significant change in color that provided the visual context for the logo the design solution kept the typestyle of the logo intact to ensure all-important continuity. Once the distinct color scheme was established we saw a dramatic change in typestyle with continuity provided by the color scheme. The point is that you should not change all elements of a logo/symbol at once, as this carries the risk of confusing consumers and disrupting the habitual buying of your existing customers.

Option 3: A great opportunity - creating a symbol that stands for the brand

When a symbol is consistently associated with a brand it will, over time, come to represent the brand, i.e., it can act as a kind of short-hand for the brand. This offers a number of benefits:
- being an image, it will be processed faster and have more impact
- a symbol is more likely to be strongly associated with certain emotions
- the symbol can be used in applications where the full logo is not practical or would detract from the message you are trying to send.

A symbol that stands for the brand is a great brand asset. It takes time to develop the strong associations required, but it is always important to look for an opportunity to create a symbol. The creation of a symbol represents a worthwhile investment into the future of the brand by creating a visual fast-track to brand recognition and to triggering the brand memory and its meaning.

From a strategic point of view, the symbol should satisfy the following criteria:
- distinct

- aligned with the logo (not just an afterthought that doesn't really integrate)
- meaningful
- have the potential to stand alone due to its distinctiveness and meaning and thus be able to represent the brand without the logo.

Triggers may include a strong, distinct color; a distinct design style, shape or image that can be brought alive; mnemonics; strap-line; jingle; and so forth.

There may also be an opportunity to use packaging design to trigger primes that have been established previously through other touchpoints. For example, a television ad or computer game may establish a prime in the consumer's mind which is triggered when exposed to the packaging. This means that, ideally, you should develop a fully integrated path-to-purchase concept that allows you to link all touchpoints through primes and triggers, adding significant firepower to your marketing spend.

Evaluating design concepts

Consumers asked to comment on package design concepts in group discussions or surveys analyze and rationalize, but consumers engaging in habitual buying don't. Habits are formed by repetition, not by a compelling argument. None of us can develop habits by simply deciding to establish them. And when we buy habitually we are simply repeating what we have done many times before without thinking. So what consumers tell you when they *think* about the design options you expose them to in research is irrelevant at best and, at worst, misleading.

You need to look at the shelf where your product is displayed in a retail outlet (e.g., supermarket) to understand which elements are key in aiding package recognition. Note that a picture or image or just seeing package designs out of context cannot substitute for the real world situation. You need to approach the shelf like a consumer would and, from a distance – using peripheral vision – see which elements make it easy to recognize your brand. This is an obligatory exercise for any marketer who wants to shape existing package design without losing habitual buyers.

When it comes to formal research there are a number of approaches you can take, including:

- You can use *eye tracking* to see where consumers look first when seeing your package on the shelf, but keep in mind that they are not likely to behave as usual once the eye tracking equipment is strapped to their head and they know that you are analyzing where they look.
- *Micro-muscle movements, brain activity or other physiological measures* that tell you how the non-conscious mind reacts to design concepts. This is a somewhat limited approach due to cost and placing consumers into an artificial environment, but it may occasionally be appropriate. (Note that micro-muscle movement measurement is now also available in a natural setting, albeit at a high cost.)
- Assessing *behavior*, by inviting consumers to pick one of several cartons to see which one they choose. By changing the context, i.e., the range of existing cartons and/or the design concepts in the mix, we can learn about the effectiveness of the new concepts. Ideally, you should carry this out in a natural environment but that's rarely possible, and using a *virtual reality store or shelf display* has proven to correlate highly with what shoppers do in a real world situation.
- Finally, you can use *predictive markets*, where consumers can invest notional money into design concepts and sell off their investments. The investment decisions made by all 'traders' determine the relative value of various design concepts. Predictive markets have been shown to be more reliable than traditional group discussions and surveys.

The most important point is that only design concepts that are aligned with your strategy should ever reach the

consumer test phase. In other words, you have to:
- Ensure that the design concept brings your chosen brand vision archetype alive. Any design concepts that do not achieve this in a compelling and meaningful way – according to your professional judgment, which is based on your understanding of the strategic requirements – have to be eliminated and should never reach the market research phase.
- If you need to retain habitual buyers of your brand you should also eliminate all design concepts that do not provide the continuity required to facilitate habitual buying.
- Finally, determine to what extent the design concept allows you to advance your key strategic initiative (for example, to create a symbol that will eventually stand as short-hand for the brand; or to incorporate primes that facilitate brand activation and shopper marketing initiatives). Your assessment will allow you to rank order design concepts so that you can eliminate the weakest ones and let only the highest ranking ones progress to consumer research.

This concludes the all-important process of design development and testing, but it is by no means the end of the package design challenge: With your design concept finalized, you have to start to integrate this touchpoint with other touchpoints. The sorts of challenges you now have to address include:
- How do you give meaning to design elements you want to associate strongly with particular qualities or attributes? How will you do this through your marketing communications, brand activations, shopper marketing initiatives?
- How can you most effectively capitalize on any primes the selected design concept incorporates? Do you plan to reinforce the prime through other touchpoints? How will you activate/trigger the prime? Where will you do this – in store or earlier along the path to purchase?
- How can you make the package redesign the focus of a marketing communications program? How can you

make this a compelling story? How, where and when will you tell this story?
- How can you support the launch of the new design? Is there anything you need to do to ensure you don't disrupt habitual buying (if that's your strategy) or to maximize the disruptive impact of the new design concept (if this is your strategy)?

There are obviously many more challenges waiting, but hopefully these examples make it obvious that package design is not an isolated activity, but needs to be addressed as part of an integrated approach to managing consumer purchases along the path to purchase.

15 Big Data and neuroscience – a marriage made in heaven?

With the growing ability to capture more data than ever before on what consumers actually do it comes as no surprise that Big Data has received a lot of attention. But what has been missing from these discussions is the meaning of the data gathered.

Traditional market research focuses on what consumers say. While observational, ethnographic and other methodologies that avoid direct questioning have been used for decades, they represent only a small share of the research dollars spent. The dominant share is spent on studies that rely – in one way or another – on questioning consumers about their attitudes, beliefs, intentions, degree of satisfaction, recall, or reactions to new products, packaging or ad concepts.

As you know, neuroscience tells us that we have two parallel systems in our mind: one designed to get us to 'do' and the other to 'think'. Traditional market research relies largely on rationalizations the consumer's conscious mind conjures up to make sense of their world. But what really drives their purchase behavior is their nonconscious mind which cannot rationalise, can't making considered choices, and can't plan ahead. This means that consumers don't know *why* they do what they do, nor can they predict with any accuracy what they will do in the future (except in case of habitual buying) because what drives their actions resides largely in their nonconscious mind.

This is not a particularly new revelation. We have known for a long time that tracking the effectiveness of a campaign on the basis of recall is at best useless and at worst misleading; that group discussions deliver opinions but rarely insights into the consumer's purchase drivers; that consumers don't think about a set of attributes when they select a brand, yet are willing to rationalize their actions when confronted with a question asking them to rate brands on a set of attributes.

But what are you to do?

While neuromarketing – the application of neuroscience insights to developing and executing marketing and communications strategies – has developed in leaps and bounds, there has always been a barrier in the research area. Sure, we can test ads or package designs in a neuroscience lab but, while this may help to improve an element of the execution, it is not going to help the marketer to make the underlying campaign strategy more effective. And, as we've already discussed, directly questioning consumers makes no sense, given that some 85% of new products fail, and the majority of these have been tested in group discussions and interviews.

So how do we get meaningful and reliable data about what is actually driving the consumer's purchase decisions? Big Data comes to the aid of neuromarketing strategists. It seems incongruous that Big Data and its focus on the behavior of the masses could complement neuroscience, which is concerned with the individual and (largely) nonconscious processes, but it is indeed a marriage made in heaven. Not least because neuromarketing addresses one of the biggest question marks hanging over Big Data: What do I do with all this information beyond planning exposures at the right place with the right message? How do I know what's really important? What am I looking for? The answer from neuromarketing is clearly: identify market segments on the basis of which goals they are seeking to address with their behavioral choices.

Thanks to Big Data we know more about what consumers actually do than ever before, while neuroscience research tells us that the consumer's purchase behavior reflects their attempts to satisfy specific, often higher level, nonconscious goals. It tells us that consumers don't buy brands because they like them, but because these brands are believed to address their goals. Big Data lets us get serious about segmenting on the basis of goals. As consumers are generally not aware of their higher level nonconscious goals, there's no point in asking them, but we can often infer these goals by looking at consumers' behavior. A simple example:

If a consumer wants adventure in their life then their behavior will reflect this. They may take adventure holidays, prefer adventure movies, spend their weekend abseiling, watch adventure TV series, choose outdoor brand casual clothing, and so forth. Naturally, adventure won't be reflected in everything they do, as money, time and the need to compromise with companions will occasionally lead to different choices but, given a diverse data set we should be able to classify this person as an adventurer without having to ask them a single question.

Much more work needs to be done to better align these two streams, but there is no doubt that a combination of Big Data that provides insights into actual behavior, with neuroscience findings on how consumers actually make purchase decisions, has the potential to revolutionize marketing as we know it today.

16 Organizational issues

Your Vision determines your goals, your goals determine your objectives, your objectives determine your strategies, and your strategies determine your organizational structure. In other words your organization should be built to facilitate, in the most effective and efficient way, the implementation of your strategies.

To illustrate this point I will consider some of the strategic challenges companies face and explore how these may impact on organizational issues.

Bridging the gap between innovation and marketing

In many organizations there is a gap between R&D/innovation and marketing. Each party is focusing on optimizing their own domain, leading to R&D taking little note of the opportunities marketing sees and vice versa. This clearly doesn't help to optimize the results for the company.

There is a need for both parties to rely on a shared approach to setting priorities, and to achieve this they must first understand the problems the company should address and, second, find innovative solutions to addressing them.

A research methodology that allows you to complete the first step – understanding the problems the company should address - in an organized, sound way is Problem Detection.

A Problem Detection study comprises of two phases: first, respondents representative of the target market are asked open ended questions about any problems they have had in the past. The focus is on what has actually happened rather than asking respondents why they thought this was a problem or if they see, or prefer, a particular solution. Consumers don't know which solutions could potentially be delivered. They don't have any idea of major trends or developments that drive innovation, nor do they understand how marketing works and what it can achieve. Any ideas for solutions would be run-of-the-mill approaches lacking an innovative, disruptive element. But they can certainly tell us about the problems they have actually experienced.

This qualitative research phase results in a problem list comprising dozens of distinct problems, typically somewhere between 80 and 120.

In the next phase, a larger sample of respondents is asked to rate each problem in terms of how important they are, and how frequently they occur. The rationale for this is that some problems occur frequently but are really not such a big deal, while others occur only very occasionally but are really annoying when they do. The combination of frequency and importance ratings provides a meaningful problem score that can be used to rank order problems for the whole sample as well as for specific segments.

This methodology enables the organization to focus on and consider only the high-ranking problems that have the potential to make a significant impact on results if a way can be found to address them effectively. The R&D or Innovation team and the marketing team will often come up with different ways of addressing a problem; this is a good thing as many problems tend to have more than one solution. What is important is that both parties are now coordinating their approach to delivering solutions to problems that are high in the consumers' rank order. Therefore the resources, expertise and experience of both parties are focused on solutions that will deliver a major impact in the market place.

Without basing the development program on a solid rank order derived through consumer research we are likely to see R&D and marketing address pet projects or problems they can see some immediate solution to. A shared rank order to guide the development process ensures alignment between the two functions as well as providing a focus on solving problems the market sees as significant.

Building global brands vs managing global brands

Managing a global brand is based on a global strategy that allows for few or no local adaptations. It is an appropriate strategy for brands that are primarily bought *because* they are global. For example, consumers all over the world buy Apple, Nike or Perrier because it they are global brands. Buying global brands can address a variety of goals, such as prestige, the excitement of belonging to a (global) group of consumers who buy that brand, a feeling of safety (as global brands are typically expected to avoid major food safety or other missteps), and so forth.

Building a global brand, on the other hand, needs to aim at increasing market share in each local market by addressing product category-related goals more effectively than competitors are seen to. Once a brand has established a significant local following it can start to make *incremental steps* towards a global strategy.

Particularly in emerging markets a global brand is likely to attract consumers simply because it is global. If that's the case it is obviously not just feasible, but highly effective, to pursue a global brand strategy. After all, the brand's positioning is based on the idea that it is successful all over the world and thus desirable, prestigious and a safe choice. It is no wonder that many of the leading global brands have found great success in China and other emerging markets.

A brand that is striving to become a global brand is in a very different position to a brand that is already established globally. It does not yet have the image – and thus advantages – a global brand can capitalize on. It follows that it will most likely be far more effective to localize its strategies to align them with the cultural and market characteristics of its major geographic markets. A global strategy is likely to be less effective as the brand has neither the credibility a global brand enjoys nor the relevance a local successful local brand can deliver by aligning itself with the local conditions.

This is all pretty obvious, yet many companies that aim

at building global brands hire senior marketing executives who have a track record in managing – rather than building – a global brand. This is despite the competencies required to build a global brand being very different to those required to manage the brand once it is global.

Agency relationships
Utilizing a variety of different communications and engagement channels and platforms typically leads to the engagement of a large number of agencies, which in turn causes fragmentation and the development and implementation of sub-optimal initiatives. However, more often than not, the reason for fragmentation and for marketers spending untold hours in meetings and presentations lies in the lack of a comprehensive brand strategy that would guide all marketing efforts.

You, as the brand owner, need to take responsibility for the development and documentation of a comprehensive brand strategy. You can use consultants or input from your agencies, but you can't delegate this responsibility. Your agencies may be great when it comes to developing an advertising, digital, PR, or engagement program but that does not make them experts in brand strategy. You should hire the best people you can find to make sure your brand strategy is effective, clear, and can be translated into the specific execution streams that will be handled by your agencies.

An agency that has a major client relationship needs to translate the brand strategy into an effective execution. I will use a creative agency as an example, but the points made apply to any agency that contributes to implementing the brand strategy. The traditional approach is to use account executives to manage the day-to-day client relationship, to keep the program on track and identify additional services that could be sold to the client. Today, there are a number of online collaboration and tracking platforms available that can take care of progress reports, scheduling, identifying the critical path, showing the impact of delays on other tasks, and so forth, while delivering full transparency.

The account executive's role needs to change from administrator to that of translating the brand strategy into an advertising strategy and ensuring that any creative, media or other recommendations are aligned with the brand strategy. This should be one of the two most important imperatives an agency has, the other being to find creative solutions to bring the brand strategy alive. Many agencies have a strategy planner or planning team, but they tend to work quite removed from the client side. My view is that an agency needs to have strategists work on a day-to-day basis with clients as this is the only way the agency can ensure that the solutions the agency delivers will in fact be aligned with the brand strategy. A one-off PowerPoint presentation by a strategy planner is not going to do the job.

Of course, I am generalizing and different clients as well as different agencies need somewhat different solutions. However, I believe the core message is relevant in all cases: the client needs to create a comprehensive, well argued, detailed, and fully documented brand strategy while the agency needs to translate this brand strategy into *an execution that will bring the strategy alive*. An agency that does this efficiently and effectively will contribute to a fully integrated marketing effort and avoid the time, effort and money traps caused by fragmentation.

17 Getting ready for the future: Artificial Intelligence

I started my introduction by highlighting the importance of being prepared for the technological revolution that is gathering pace. It seems fitting to end with one of the technologies that is already making an impact in marketing and is destined to increase in importance: Artificial Intelligence.

There is no 'universal' AI. In fact, while experts are working towards an Artificial *General* Intelligence solution – an AI engine that can address different problems just like a human mind – today we have to use different AI solutions for different types of problems.

To illustrate this point, take the example of a digital assistant managing customer inquiries on a web site. The AI engine needs to assess the context of the inquiry and even the mood of the inquirer to fully understand the challenge, select the answer from a knowledge bank, and deliver this answer in a form that is appropriate given context and mood. Essential AI capabilities include language and pattern recognition, matching patterns, and managing a knowledge/experience base.

In contrast consider an application where you want to optimize a media schedule or shopper marketing initiatives. You are facing an almost infinite number of combinations and permutations and AI needs to optimize your choices, may these be content delivered via certain media or shopper marketing initiatives via in-store touchpoints. A back propagation artificial neural network AI is the appropriate choice here – a very different type of AI than in the previous example. As the name suggests, such an AI engine simulates a neural network that learns from each application, adapts the existing neural network to accommodate new sets of input variables, and thus is able to optimize an ever-increasing range of different input constellations.

Back propagation artificial neural networks – the AI engines typically used for optimization challenges - have to be trained. That is, they start being quite ignorant and delivering sub-standard optimization recommendations but learn from every application and, given extensive, clean training data, within a few months deliver optimization results that are better than those generated by traditional methods such as econometric models.

Common problems when adopting AI
Every week – if not every day – organizations decide they want to adopt AI to optimize some of their processes, generate more accurate projections or guide strategic decisions. There are a number of common pitfalls that need to be considered to ensure you can avoid them.

Understanding where AI can be effectively utilized
All too often a vague idea prevails that AI is some sort of magical black box that can optimize just about everything. Little thought is given to where AI can be effectively utilized, what risks AI optimization brings, how optimization of a particular aspect of the operation might create undesirable effects elsewhere, how long the pay-back period might be, or whether the AI optimization would in fact contribute to your competitive advantage.

What you need to do is explore potential AI applications, decide on a set of criteria and prioritize these applications. The criteria may change as you gain more expertise in managing AI projects. Early on, it may be appropriate to look for projects that can deliver a return in the short-term, while later on the focus might shift to give priority to applications that will contribute most effectively to building a long-term competitive advantage.

Clear optimization objectives
When it comes to optimization one of the key challenges is to set clear objectives and parameters. Unless these are

clearly defined and aligned with strategic imperatives you may end up with AI-based recommendations that result in major setbacks or even catastrophes.

A classic illustration is a defence research center challenging AI to find the optimum strategy for the commander of a naval escort taking a convoy through waters controlled by enemy submarines (told by Tony Budd in *The Economist*, February 17th, 2018). When they simulated actual convoys from World War II they found that AI achieved fewer losses and faster travel times than had actually happened. When they examined the results to understand why this was so, they found that in each case the AI solution dispatched a destroyer to sink the slowest merchant ship in the convoy to speed up progress!

Having clean data or no data at all....
All too often organizations point to a massive data lake, assuming that massive data means AI can be applied successfully. However, you have to make sure that relevant and clean data is provided and that you have the breadth of data required to generate effective AI solutions.

Voice recognition (today a key element of many AI systems such as customer service applications and personal digital assistants) can serve as an example. For years, experts struggled to develop voice recognition systems that work with a majority of people. The breakthrough came when companies recording customer phone inquiries – which the customer was told would be recorded for training purposes – sold these recordings to firms working on voice recognition systems. Having recordings of tens of millions of *different* people allowed AI engines to develop a highly effective voice recognition system.

However, having said that, you don't need any historical data as long as you generate a massive data flow moving forward that can be used to train your AI engine. Of course, the early optimization results your AI engine delivers will be sub-optimal until it has learned from real life cases. But progress is typically fast and soon AI will overtake the quality delivered by other approaches to optimization, including human judgment.

Trusting the AI engine's optimization recommendations

Management often assumes that they can check an AI recommendation or projection, i.e., assess its underlying rationale or the logic it is based on. This is not the case. AI will deliver an optimization result or projection, but it cannot explain how the output was derived. Moreover, each case can change the digital neural network AI is using which would make it impossible to keep track of how solutions were derived, even if you could understand the AI's neural network – which you can't! In other words, you need to ask yourself if you trust the AI engine sufficiently to follow the optimized recommendations or act on the projections it has delivered. To underline the importance of this question, refer back to the naval defence example I have just cited.

About the author

Dr Peter Steidl has lived in Austria, Germany, the United Kingdom and Australia and has carried out assignments in more than 20 countries on five continents. His clients include a number of Fortune Global 100 corporations, start-up companies, professional services firms, federal and state government agencies and not-for-profit organizations.

Peter has an MBA and PhD from Vienna University and has served on the permanent staff of Vienna and Adelaide University, taught in the MBA program and held a Visiting Adjunct Professorship at Curtin University in Perth.

He has been a Temporary Advisor to the World Health Organization, has represented Australia at the European Center for Social Science Research and Documentation, served as Honorary Austrian Consul for South Australia and the Northern Territory and has served on government boards and committees as well as on the boards of not-for-profit organizations.

He has conducted workshops and seminars and delivered keynote addresses and papers at international and local conferences, and has conducted staff development programs with agencies and client marketing departments.

Peter is a prolific writer. His most recent books include: Paul Dovas, Peter Steidl, et. al., *Market Research Revolution. A Marketer's Guide To Emerging New Methods*, NMSBA, 2017; Peter Steidl, *The Book Of Change: Make the Changes You Want, And Make Them Stick*, Createspace, 2017; Peter Steidl, *Neuromarketing Essentials: What Every Marketer Needs To Know*, NMSBA, 2016; MacInnes Carl & Peter Steidl, *Shopper Marketing. Winning the Battle at the Shelf*, NMSBA, 2016; Boehm Kim & Peter Steidl, *Brand Vision Archetypes: Creating Brands With Meaning*, NMSBA, 2016; Peter Steidl, *Smarter, Wiser, Calmer, Focused: Your Brain's Natural Advantage*, Createspace, 2016

Peter can be contacted at **peter@neurothinking.com** or via Linkedin.

References

The Classic

Kahneman, Daniel — *Thinking, Fast and Slow*, FSG, 2011

Introductory Texts

Genco, Stephen J. & Andrew P. Pohlmann Peter Steidl — *Neuromarketing for Dummies*, Wiley & &Sons 2013

Steidl, Peter — *Neuromarketing Essentials. What Every Marketer Needs To Know*, NMSBA, 2016

Weber, Daryl — *Brand Seduction. How Neuroscience Can Help Marketers Build Memorable Brands*, Career Press, 2016

Consumer Behavior, Goals, DRDs

Ariely, Dan — *Predictable Irrationality: The Hidden Forces that Shape Our Decisions*, Harper 2009

Brafman, Ori — *Sway:The Irresistible Pull of Irrational Behavior*, Doubleday 2008

Dooley, Roger — *Brainfluence: 100 Ways to Persuade and Convince Consumers with Neuromarketing*, Wiley & Sons 2012

Johnson, Steven — *Everything Bad is Good for You*, Penguin 2006

Lawrence, Paul R. & Nitin Nohria — *Driven: How Human Nature Shapes Our Choices*, Jossey-Bass 2002

Lieberman, Matthew D. — *Social. Why Our Brains Are Wired to Connect*, Crown Publishers, 2013

Martin, Neale — *Habit: The 95% of Behavior Marketers Ignore*, Pearson Education 2008

Pink, Daniel H. — *Drive: The Surprising Truth about What Motivates Us*, Riverhead Books 2009

Steidl, Peter — *Smarter, Wiser, Calmer, Focused. Your Brain's Natural Advantage*, 2016

Impact of Digital Revolution on the Brain

Carr, Nicholas	*The Shallows. What the Internet is Doing to Our Brains*, W. W. Norton 2011
Gardner, Howard & Katie Davis	*The App Generation*, Yale University Press, 2013
Keen, Andrew	*The Cult of the Amateur. How Today's Internet is Killing Our Culture and Assaulting Our Economy*, 2007
Pollack, Stefan	*Disrupted. From Gen Y to iGen*, Pacific Coast Creative Publishing 2013
Toyama, Kentaro	*Geek Heresy. Rescuing Social Change From The Cult Of Technology*, Perseus, 2015
Watson, Richard	*Future Minds: How the Digital Age is Changing Our Minds, Why This Matters and What We Can Do About It*, Nicholas Brealey 2010

Behavioral Economics

Altman, Morris	*Behavioral Economics for Dummies*, Wiley & Sons, 2012
Thaler, Richard H. Cass R. Sunstein	*Nudge. Improving Decisions About Health, Wealth, and Happiness*, Penguin, 2009
Thaler, Richard H.	*Misbehaving. The Making Of Behavioral Economics*, W. W. Norton, 2015

Disruption Strategies

Dru, Jean-Marie	*Beyond Disruption*, Adweek 2002
Duggan, William	*Strategic Intuition. The Creative Spark in Human Achievement*, Columbia University Press 2007
Frankl, Viktor E.	*Man's Search for Meaning*, Simon & Schuster 1984
Gans, Joshua	*The Disruption Dilemma*, MIT Press, 2016

Holt, Douglas	*Cultural Strategy. Using Innovative Ideologies to Build Breakthrough Brands,*
& Douglas Cameron	Oxford Press 2010
Kim, W. Chan & Renee Mauborgne	*Blue Ocean Strategy. How to Create Uncontested Market Space and Make the Competition Irrelevant,* Harvard Business Review Press, 2005
Kim, W. Chan & Renee Mauborgne	*Blue Ocean Shift Beyond Competing. Proven Steps To Inspire Confidence And Seize New Growth,* Hachette, 2017
Steidl, Peter	*Survive, Exploit, Disrupt. Action Guidelines for Marketing in a Recession,* John Wiley & Sons, 2009
Thinius, Jochen & Jan Untiedt	*Events – Erlebnismarketing fuer alle Sinne. Mit neuronaler Marketkommunikation Lebensstile Inszenieren,* 2nd ed., Springer 2017
Verganti, Roberto	*Design-Driven Innovation. Changing the Rules of Competition by Radically Innovating What Things Mean,* Harvard Business Press, 2009

Brand Vision Archetypes

Boehm Kim & Peter Steidl	*Brand Vision Archetypes: Creating Brands with Meaning,* NMSBA, 2016
Campbell, Joseph	*Transformation of Myth Through Time,* Harper Perennial 1999
Campbell, Joseph	*Myths of Light: Eastern Metaphors of the Eternal,* New World Library 2003
Jung, Carl G	*The Archetypes and the Collective Unconscious,* Princeton Univ. Press 1990

Marketing Communications and Design
Here I have included books that primarily use marketing communications examples

Barden, Phil — *Decoded. The Science Behind Why We Buy*, Wiley & Sons 2013

Note: this book includes essential elements of a range of German books: Christian Scheier et. al., *Wie Werbung Wirkt: Erkenntnisse des Neuromarketing*, 2010; *Was Marken Erfolgreich Macht: Neuropsychologie in der Markenfuehrung* 2009, and *Codes: Die Geheime Sprache der Produkte*, 2010.

Pradeep, A. K. — *The Buying Brain. Secrets for Selling to the Subconscious Mind*, John Wiley & Sons, 2010

Willcox, Matthew — *The Business Of Choice. Marketing To Consumers' Instincts*, Pearson 2015

Shopper Marketing

MacInnes Carl & Peter Steidl — Shopper Marketing. Winning the Battle at the Shelf, NMSBA, 2016

Market Research, Insights

Bridger, Darren — *Decoding The Irrational Consumer. How To Commission, Run And Generate Insights From Neuromarketing Research*, Kogan

Du Plessis, Erik — *The Branded Mind: What Neuroscience Really Tells Us about the Puzzle of the Brain and the Brand*, Kogan Page 2007

Klein, Gary — *Seeing What Others Don't*, Nicholas Braeley Publishing 2014

Paul Dovas et. al. — *Market Research Revolution. A Marketer's Guide To Emerging New Methods*, NMSBA, 2017

Zaltman, Gerald — *How Customers Think. Essential Insights into the Mind of the Market*, Harvard Business School Press, 2003

Other valuable books...

Amthor, Frank — *Neuroscience for Dummies*, Wiley & Sons, 2012

Doidge, Norman	*The Brain that Changes Itself*, Viking Penguin 2007
Earls, Mark	*Herd. How to Change Mass Behavior by Harnessing Our True Nature*, John Wiley & Sons 2009
Georges, Patrick M. et. al.	*Neuromarketing In Action. How To Talk And Sell To The Brain*, Kogan Page, 2014
Hammond, Claudia	*Emotional Rollercoaster. A Journey through the Science of Feelings*, Harper Perennial 2006
Lehrer, Jonah	*The Decisive Moment. How the Brain Makes Up Its Mind*, Text, 2009
Mlodinow, Leonard	*Subliminal. How Your Unconscious Mind Rules Your Behavior*, Random House, 2012
Schwartz, Barry	*The Paradox of Choice: Why More is Less. How the Culture of Abundance Robs Us of Satisfaction*, Harper Perennial 2004
Wilson, Timothy D.	*Redirect. The Surprising New Science of Psychological Change*, Little Brown, 2011

Made in the USA
Las Vegas, NV
01 November 2023